AF413240

Voices:

Linguistic and Cultural Dynamics of Refugee Population in America

Written By

Paarth Mathur

Paarth Mathur

Dedication

To my cherished grandparents

Paarth Mathur

Acknowledgment

Writing this book has been a journey of discovery, reflection, and growth, and I am deeply grateful to the many people who have supported me along the way.

First and foremost, I would like to thank my grandparents, whose stories and teachings have profoundly influenced my understanding of culture and history. Your love of learning and sharing knowledge has been a constant source of inspiration.

To my parents, thank you for your endless support, encouragement, and belief in my abilities.

Your guidance and values have shaped the person I am today, and this book would not have been possible without your influence.

I would also like to extend my heartfelt thanks to my teachers and mentors, who have nurtured my passion for learning and provided invaluable insights during this process. Your dedication to education and your belief in the power of knowledge have driven me to explore and understand the complexities of linguistic and cultural dynamics.

A special thanks to the refugee communities I have had the privilege of working with. Your resilience, stories, and experiences have deeply impacted me, and I hope this book does justice to your incredible journeys.

Lastly, to my friends and colleagues who have offered their time, feedback, and support throughout this project—thank you for your encouragement and for believing in the importance of this work.

This book is a culmination of many voices, experiences, and lessons learned. I am grateful to each and every one of you for your contribution to this endeavor.

Voices: Linguistic and Cultural Dynamics of Refugee Population in America

"It's important that the U.S. remains a leader in all refugee matters, including resettlement. It is a humanitarian matter, and this leadership must continue."

-FILIPPO GRANDI, UNITED NATIONS HIGH COMMISSIONER FOR REFUGEE

Paarth Mathur

Preface

The term **"Vasudhaiva Kutumbakam"** is a Sanskrit phrase that translates to "the world is one family" in English. It is a philosophical concept often cited to express the idea of the interconnectedness of all living beings and the importance of treating the world as a global family. The concept emphasizes the need for compassion, empathy, and a sense of shared responsibility toward all individuals, transcending geographical, cultural, and religious boundaries.

The phrase is a profound expression of the interconnectedness of all living beings and the oneness of humanity. It conveys the idea that the entire world is like a single family where individuals are interconnected and interdependent. It promotes the concept of universal brotherhood, emphasizing that we should treat everyone with love, compassion, and understanding, regardless of differences such as race, religion, nationality, or social status. It advocates for a sense of global responsibility and harmony, suggesting that the well-being of one is intricately linked to the well-being of all.

This concept has been embraced in various forms across different cultures and religions, reflecting a universal aspiration for peace, cooperation, and unity. It serves as a reminder to foster a sense of empathy and interconnectedness in our interactions with others, both locally and globally. Advocates of the **"Vasudhaiva Kutumbakam"** philosophy argue that it is not enough for individual nations to focus solely on their own interests. Instead, they believe that a more compassionate and interconnected approach is needed, where countries work together to provide assistance, support, and refuge to those in need, irrespective of national borders.

The phenomenon of globalization, while characterized by an unprecedented exchange of technology, cultures, food, language, and trade, reveals a glaring asymmetry when confronted with collaborative responses to humanitarian crises. On one hand, the interconnectedness

vi

Voices: Linguistic and Cultural Dynamics of Refugee Population in America

facilitated by technological advancements has propelled the rapid dissemination of ideas, fostered a rich tapestry of global cultures, and facilitated international trade. The fusion of diverse culinary traditions, the widespread sharing of information, and the ease of cross-cultural communication have created a world that, in many ways, seems like a closely-knit global family. However, this interconnectedness stands in stark contrast to the inadequacies and inefficiencies in addressing collaborative humanitarian challenges.

The world's response to crises such as pandemics, natural disasters, and refugee displacement often exposes the shortcomings of a truly unified global approach. Despite the shared vulnerabilities to issues like climate change and public health crises, nations often grapple with internal interests and geopolitical considerations that hinder swift and coordinated responses. Humanitarian aid is frequently marred by bureaucratic hurdles, political tensions, and a lack of collective commitment. The disproportionate burden placed on certain regions exacerbates disparities, highlighting the unequal distribution of resources and capabilities among nations. The absence of a seamless and collaborative global humanitarian strategy underscores the lopsided nature of globalization, revealing a world that, despite its interconnectivity, struggles to prioritize collective well-being over individual interests.

To address this disparity, there is a pressing need for increased international cooperation, strengthened institutional frameworks, and a reevaluation of priorities to place humanitarian concerns at the forefront of global decision-making. Only through a more balanced and inclusive approach can globalization truly fulfill its potential as a force for positive transformation, ensuring that the benefits of interconnectedness extend to all, especially in times of shared human challenges.

My book **"Voices: Linguistic and Cultural Dynamics of the Refugee Population in the United States"** beautifully captures the reciprocal nature of community engagement, where the initial goal of providing assistance transforms into a shared journey of learning, understanding, and personal development. It's a powerful reminder of the richness that comes from connecting with and supporting others.

Voices: Linguistic and Cultural Dynamics of Refugee Population in America

Table of Contents

Dedication iii

Acknowledgment iv

Preface vi

Chapter 1 13

History of the 1951 Convention 14

Refugee Act of 1980 17

Chapter 2 24

Natural Evolution of Languages: 26

Types of Language Change: 26

Causes of Linguistic Evolution: 27

Language Evolution in Action: 27

Studying Linguistic Evolution: 28

The Role of Language Preservation: 28

Chapter 3 Language Diversity and English Proficiency 30

The Limited English Proficient Population 33

Distribution by State and Key Cities 33

Nativity 35

Language Diversity 37

Age, Race, and Ethnicity 39

Education and Employment 40

Poverty 41

Chapter 4 The Language of the Unspoken 44

A Multifaceted Linguistic Landscape: 44

Global Distribution of Sign Languages: 45

Examples of Sign Languages: 45

Refugee crises: A journey of Understanding 49

A Baby Shower to remember. 51

Chapter 5 Cultural Diversity: America a Global Leader 55

Frank Sinatra 57

Is U.S. Falling Short of Refugees Expectations as a Global Leader 61

Chapter 6 Integration Barriers: Perspectives from Refugee Youth .. 66

Cultural Adaptation and Integration: A Phased Approach 70

Integration Challenges of Refugee Population 75

Chapter 7 Linguistic Challenges 81

Building Meaningful Refugee 83

Integration or Coercion? 89

Autonomous Agency 90

Balancing Integration and Autonomy 90

Opportunities 92

What factors can erode public support and cause compassion fatigue?. 99

Perception of lack of control over migration 104

Sense of existential threat 105

Conclusion 106

Appendix 115

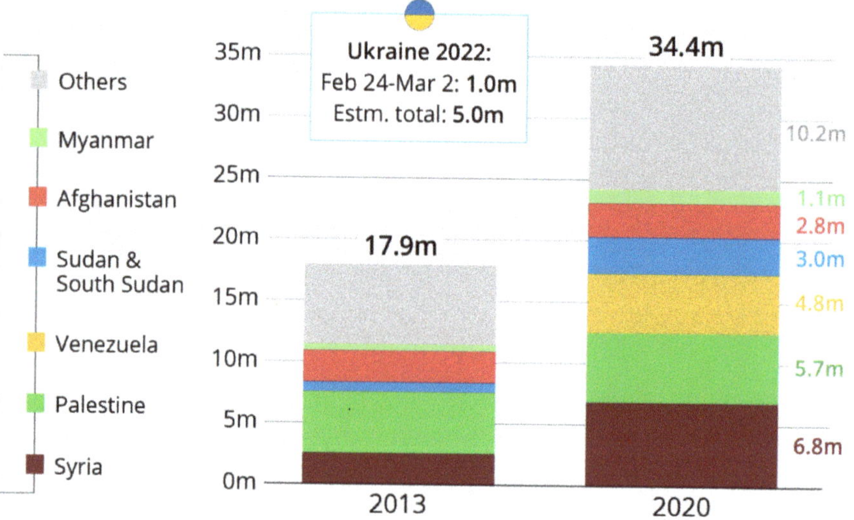
The World's Refugee Crises
Number of internationally displaced people
by country of origin*
Others
Myanmar
Afghanistan
Sudan &
South Sudan
Venezuela
Palestine
Syria
35m
30m
25m
20m
15m
10m
5m
0m
Ukraine 2022:
Feb 24-Mar 2: 1.0m
Estm. total: 5.0m
34.4m
10.2m
1.1m
2.8m
3.0m
4.8m
5.7m
6.8m
17.9m
2013
2020
* includes refugees, asylum-seekers and Venezuelans abroad
Sources: UNHCR, U.S. Mission to the UN

Chapter 1

In the aftermath of World War II, the world witnessed a surge in displaced populations, and the year 1951 marked a critical period for refugees seeking a new beginning. Among them was a family of three – the Al-Mansours, who found themselves caught in the tumultuous currents of post-war Europe.

Fleeing their war-torn homeland in the Middle East, the Al-Mansours embarked on a perilous journey across borders, seeking refuge and solace. The war had left them with scars, both physical and emotional, and they dreamt of a place where they could rebuild their shattered lives.

Their odyssey led them to a refugee camp in Germany, a temporary haven where countless families sought asylum. The camp, though a far cry from the warmth of home, became a melting pot of cultures, languages, and shared dreams. It was here that the Al-Mansours forged unexpected bonds with people from diverse backgrounds, each carrying their tales of resilience and survival.

The year 1951 marked the establishment of the United Nations Convention Relating to the Status of Refugees, a beacon of hope for those yearning for a stable future. The Al-Mansours, like many others, were granted refugee status under this historic convention. It was a document that promised protection, rights, and the possibility of a fresh start.

Their journey continued as they were resettled in a small town in the United States. The Al-Mansours faced the challenges of adapting to a new culture, learning a new language, and building a life from scratch. Yet, in the face of adversity, they found a supportive community that embraced their resilience and welcomed them with open arms.

The fate of refugees around 1951 was one of both struggle and hope. The establishment of international conventions marked a turning point, offering a framework for protecting the rights of those forced to flee their homes. For the Al-Mansours and countless others, 1951 was a chapter of survival, adaptation, and the gradual restoration of a sense of home in a world still grappling with the scars of war.

History of the 1951 Convention

In the aftermath of the First World War (1914 - 1918), millions of people fled their homelands in search of refuge. Governments responded by drawing up a set of international agreements to provide travel documents for these people who were, effectively, the first recognized refugees of the 20th century. Their numbers increased dramatically during and after the Second World War (1939-1945), as millions more were forcibly displaced.

In response, the international community steadily assembled a set of guidelines, laws, and conventions aimed at protecting basic human rights and treating people forced to flee conflict and persecution.

The process, which began under the League of Nations in 1921, culminated in the 1951 Convention, which consolidated and expanded on previous international instruments relating to refugees and continues to provide the most comprehensive codification of the rights of refugees at the international level.

In July 1951, a diplomatic conference in Geneva adopted the Convention Relating to the Status of Refugees. It has since been subject to only one amendment in the form of the 1967 Protocol.

Initially, the 1951 Convention was essentially limited to protecting European refugees in the aftermath of the Second World War: The document contains the words "events occurring before 1 January 1951," which are widely understood to mean "events occurring in Europe" prior to that date.

The 1967 Protocol, adopted on 4 October 1967, removes these geographic and time-based limitations, expanding the Convention to apply universally and protect all persons fleeing conflict and persecution.

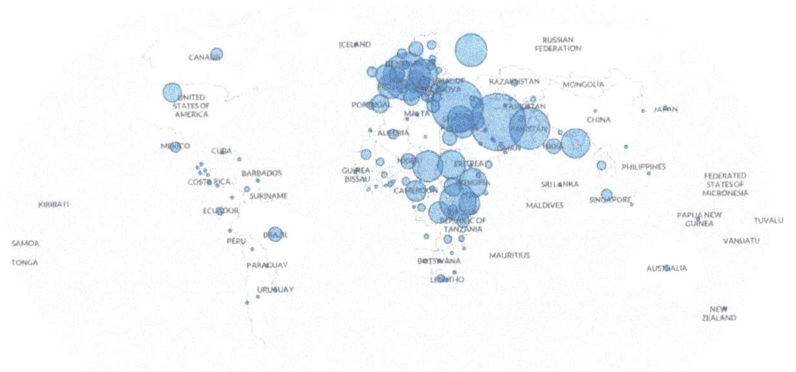

World map of forcibly displaced stateless people

The terms asylum seeker, refugee, internally displaced people (IDPs), stateless people, and returnees encapsulate distinct categories within the realm of forced migration and displacement.

An asylum seeker is an individual who has fled their home country due to well-founded fears of persecution based on factors such as race, religion, nationality, membership in a particular social group, or political opinion.

Asylum is the protection granted to foreign nationals already in the United States or arriving at the border who meet the international law definition of a "refugee." The United Nations 1951 Convention and 1967 Protocol define a *refugee* as a person who is unable or unwilling to return to his or her home country and cannot obtain protection in that country due to past persecution or a well-founded fear of being persecuted in the future "on account of race, religion, nationality, membership in a particular social group, or political opinion." Congress incorporated this definition into U.S. immigration law in the Refugee Act of 1980. Asylum is technically a "discretionary" status, meaning that some individuals can be denied asylum even if they meet the definition of a refugee. For those individuals, a backstop form of protection known as "withholding of removal" may be available to protect them from harm if necessary. Seeking asylum involves requesting protection and refuge in another country but does not guarantee automatic recognition as a refugee.

As a signatory to the 1967 Protocol, and through U.S. immigration law, the United States has legal obligations to provide protection to those who qualify as refugees. The Refugee Act established two paths to obtain refugee status—either from abroad as a resettled refugee or in the United States as an asylum seeker.

Refugees are individuals who have been officially recognized as having a well-founded fear of persecution and have sought international protection. They have crossed international borders and cannot or are unwilling to return to their home country due to the risk of persecution. Refugees often receive legal recognition and assistance from host countries and international organizations.

Internally displaced people (IDPs) are individuals who have been forced to flee their homes but remain within the borders of their own country. Unlike refugees, IDPs have not crossed international borders and may face challenges in accessing protection and assistance, as their displacement is often within the jurisdiction of their own government.

Stateless people are individuals who are not recognized as citizens by any country. They lack the protection and rights associated with citizenship, making them vulnerable to discrimination and restricted access to essential services. Statelessness can result from various factors, including gaps in nationality laws or the breakup of states.

Returnees are individuals who, after displacement, voluntarily return to their home country or region. This process may occur when conditions in the home country improve, facilitating the safe and sustainable return of individuals who had previously sought refuge elsewhere. Returnees may face challenges such as rebuilding their lives and communities, and the success of returns often depends on the stability and security of the home country.

These definitions highlight the diverse circumstances and legal considerations associated with individuals affected by forced migration, emphasizing the need for tailored responses to address the unique challenges faced by asylum seekers, refugees, IDPs, stateless people, and returnees.

The definition of a refugee originates from the 1951 Refugee Convention, in which a refugee is defined as someone who has a well-founded fear of persecution for reasons of race, religion, nationality, political opinion, or membership in a particular social group.

Presently, millions of individuals globally have been compelled to abandon their residences in a bid to escape the ravages of civil conflict and other forms of violence. Recent data from the United Nations reveals staggering figures, with 22.5 million classified as refugees and an additional 38 million identified as internally displaced persons (IDPs). Remarkably, statistical trends from 1996 to 2016 indicate that refugee numbers have reached a two-decade pinnacle. Simultaneously, internal displacement, denoting the forced evacuation of individuals from their homes without crossing international borders, has also reached a twenty-year high.

Refugee Act of 1980

In the aftermath of the Vietnam War, the need for a change in American policy concerning refugees became apparent as hundreds of thousands of Vietnamese and Cambodians fled political chaos and physical danger in their homelands. Between 1975 and 1979, some 300,000 of these refugees were able to come to the United States through Presidential action, as the law at the time restricted refugee admissions. Seeing this, many members of Congress wanted to establish a more regular system of immigration and resettlement that would establish a clear and flexible policy.

Passed unanimously by the Senate in late 1979 and signed into law by President Jimmy Carter in early 1980, the Refugee Act of 1980 amended the earlier Immigration and Nationality Act and the Migration and Refugee Assistance Act. It raised the annual ceiling for refugees from 17,400 to 50,000, created a process for reviewing and adjusting the refugee ceiling to meet emergencies, and required annual consultation between Congress and the President.

The Act also changed the definition of "refugee" to a person with a "well-founded fear of persecution," a standard established by United Nations conventions and protocols. It also funded a new Office of U.S. Coordinator for Refugee Affairs and an Office of Refugee Resettlement and built on already existing public-private partnerships that helped refugees settle and adjust to life in their new country.

A notable aspect is that 55 percent of the world's refugees originate from three states mired in prolonged civil wars: Syria (5.5 million), Somalia (1.4 million), and Afghanistan (2.5 million).

Contrary to the hopeful anticipation of safety in new locations, many displaced individuals continue to face security threats. The exploitation of refugee groups for political and strategic gains not only compromises their safety but also diminishes the gravity of the human suffering entwined with the crisis. Beyond being a tragic consequence of civil conflict, colossal and seemingly insurmountable refugee crises often become entangled in the complex web of political, security, and economic dimensions of the conflict. Initial responses to refugee influxes typically focus on practical concerns, such as meeting basic needs and organizing displacement logistics, with limited direct involvement from national political leaders. However, as the crisis expands geographically and numerically, leaders are compelled to confront broader implications, although the discourse often emphasizes the humanitarian disaster rather than the conflict itself, inadvertently increasing the likelihood of scapegoating and manipulation. Temporary situations take on the appearance of permanence, heightening displacement-related tensions within and between affected states and diverting attention from conflict resolution.

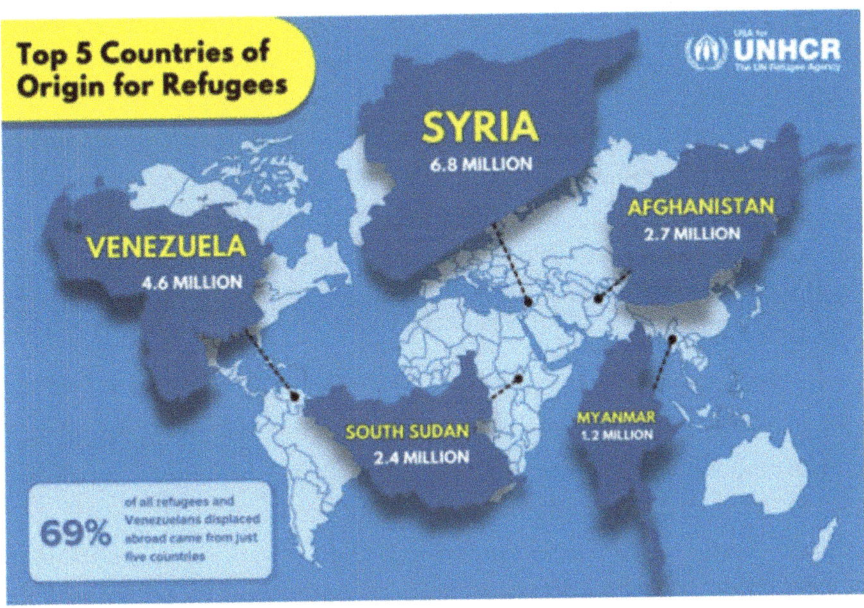

The destabilizing effects of substantial refugee populations are a major concern for many host states, straining their resources as well as those of the refugees and international donors. Governing parties, fearing a potential loss of power due to public discontent over economic hardships and social pressures linked to large refugee populations, may experience exacerbated political, ethnic, or religious tensions within the host state or with sending states. In Lebanon, a country already facing political and economic turmoil, Syrian refugees now account for over 20 percent of the population. This influx is often blamed for the increase in food and housing costs and the decrease in wages. The presence of these predominantly Sunni Arab refugees also affects the country's fragile sectarian equilibrium, impacting Christian and Shia Muslim communities. Lebanese authorities, fearing the risk

Voices: Linguistic and Cultural Dynamics of Refugee Population in America

of conflict, have taken strict security measures against refugees, including conducting raids and making arrests. Countries bearing the immediate impact of such crises feel a sense of betrayal when wealthier nations decline to accept even a minimal number of displaced people. This situation has led some regional governments to use refugees as bargaining chips in talks with Western countries, trying to avoid a large-scale arrival of asylum seekers. Humanitarian organizations, refugees, and supportive governments have strongly criticized the use of displaced people for political purposes, particularly actions that violate international refugee protection laws. In extreme cases, host countries overwhelmed or unwelcoming may cut back on legal protections and aid, causing violence and further displacement, as observed in the large-scale migration from the Middle East to Europe.

Turning to the United States, Latinos have become the largest ethnic group in Texas, surpassing non-Hispanic whites in population numbers, according to the U.S. Census Bureau. Despite representing 40.2% of the state's population and edging out the non-Hispanic white population at 39.8%, Latino political influence has yet to match their demographic strength. Factors such as unfamiliarity with the U.S. electoral system, government-related paperwork apprehensions, and discriminatory practices like voter ID laws that disproportionately affect Latinos hinder their political participation. Additionally, redistricting efforts have been manipulated to dilute their voting power. Despite these challenges, the future of Texas is increasingly tied to the prosperity and social advancement of its Latino population. The state's well-being hinges on enabling Latinos to achieve their full potential in the years ahead.

The integration of refugees enriches host societies with a tapestry of linguistic and cultural diversity, sparking innovation, economic growth, and a deeper understanding among communities. By bringing unique traditions, skills, and perspectives, refugees contribute to the social fabric in myriad ways, from enhancing the arts and cuisine to fueling business innovation and enriching educational environments. Government policies aimed at supporting refugees' integration are crucial, as they not only help individuals rebuild their lives but also unlock the potential benefits of diversity for the broader society. Such policies should focus on language education, employment opportunities, and access to health and social services, fostering an environment where both refugees and host communities can thrive together in mutual respect and cooperation.

The first chapter, titled "Language as an Identity," sets out to explore the profound impact that the movement of displaced populations has on the world's linguistic diversity. Through the lens of refugee experiences, we delve into a comprehensive examination of how these shifts contribute to the intricate mosaic of global languages. This journey not only uncovers the role of language in shaping identity but also showcases the significant ways in which refugees enrich linguistic landscapes across the globe. This chapter delves into the complexities and nuances of linguistic diversity brought about by refugees, illuminating how their languages reflect not only a means of communication but also a repository of culture, identity, and history. As we navigate through the pages, we uncover the challenges refugees face in preserving their native languages while adapting to new linguistic environments. Simultaneously, we celebrate the opportunities this diversity presents for host communities, from fostering cross-cultural understanding to enriching the linguistic landscape. Through a blend of personal narratives, theoretical insights, and practical examples, this chapter aims to highlight the significance of linguistic diversity in shaping more inclusive, resilient, and vibrant societies. By recognizing and valuing the linguistic contributions of refugees, we can better appreciate the complex interplay between language, identity, and displacement, paving the way for policies and practices that support both integration and the preservation of linguistic heritage.

Voices: Linguistic and Cultural Dynamics of Refugee Population in America

Language as an identity

Language, as a vessel of culture, identity, and history, plays a pivotal role in the lives of migrants, immigrants, and refugees. It stands at the heart of many discussions surrounding migration and integration, carrying with it the power to both include and exclude, to empower and disenfranchise. This chapter delves into how the movement of these groups has reshaped the linguistic landscape of our world, creating a tapestry of languages that narrates the complex story of human migration.

Paarth Mathur

Language is being extensively used, many times with specific intent, to stigmatize those crossing borders

Chapter 2

For migrants, immigrants, and refugees, language serves as a key to unlock new opportunities in their host countries. It's often seen as a critical tool for integration, enabling access to education, employment, and social networks. However, the journey of acquiring a new language comes with its challenges, from the practical difficulties of learning to the emotional weight of potentially losing touch with one's mother tongue. Despite these hurdles, the linguistic diversity migrants bring to their new homes enriches the cultural and social fabric of these societies.

Refugee communities often bring a rich tapestry of languages and dialects to their host countries. This linguistic diversity is not only a testament to the global nature of refugee movements but also highlights the varied cultural backgrounds and histories of these populations. Multilingualism within these communities can serve as a crucial resource, enabling communication, mutual support, and the maintenance of cultural identity.

For many refugees, the language of their host country represents a significant barrier to integration. Difficulties in communication can hinder access to vital services, including education, healthcare, and legal assistance. The challenge of learning a new language while coping with the trauma of displacement and the pressures of resettlement can be daunting, impacting refugees' ability to adapt and thrive in their new environments.

Language learning is a critical aspect of the adaptation process for refugees. It not only facilitates access to opportunities and services but also plays a significant role in the social integration process. Learning the host country's language enables refugees to build connections with the local community, participate in social and cultural activities, and contribute to their new societies. Educational programs and language courses are vital in supporting refugees through this process, although access to such resources can vary widely.

While learning the host country's language is important, the maintenance of heritage languages within refugee communities is equally significant. These languages are integral to cultural identity, heritage, and the transmission of cultural values and traditions to younger generations. Bilingualism and multilingualism are common within refugee communities, with individuals often navigating multiple linguistic identities.

Cities across the globe, from New York to Melbourne, bear witness to the incredible impact of migration on linguistic diversity. Neighborhoods bustling with the sounds of dozens of languages serve as living museums of humanity's rich cultural heritage. These linguistic landscapes offer a mosaic of stories, traditions, and histories, each adding a unique thread to the cultural tapestry of their new homes. This diversity not only enriches the cultural life of communities but also fosters greater understanding and tolerance among different ethnic groups.

Language is a dynamic and ever-evolving system of communication that shapes and reflects the culture, history, and societal developments of a particular group of speakers. Just like biological evolution, languages undergo a process of change over time, known as linguistic evolution. This phenomenon encompasses a variety of factors that contribute to the transformation of languages, including phonological shifts, grammatical changes, lexical additions and losses, and alterations in syntax and semantics. The study of linguistic evolution not only sheds light on the intricate mechanisms driving language change but also provides valuable insights into the social and historical contexts that influence these shifts.

Natural Evolution of Languages:

Linguistic evolution is a natural process that occurs as a result of various factors, such as cultural interactions, technological advancements, migration, and even generational differences. These influences gradually reshape languages, leading to the creation of new linguistic features while older elements become obsolete or transform into something new. Just as species evolve over time due to environmental pressures, languages adapt to the changing needs and contexts of their speakers.

Types of Language Change:

Linguistic evolution encompasses different types of language change:

Phonological Changes: These involve alterations in the pronunciation of sounds within a language. Over time, shifts in pronunciation can lead to changes in vowel and consonant patterns, which ultimately affect the overall phonetic makeup of a language.

Grammatical Changes: Changes in the structure of a language's grammar can occur, affecting word order, tense, aspect, mood, and other grammatical features. These changes often reflect shifts in how speakers conceptualize time, agency, and relationships.

Lexical Changes: New words are constantly being introduced into languages through various means, such as borrowing from other languages, coining new terms, and repurposing existing words. At the same time, certain words might fall out of use or take on new meanings.

Semantic Changes: Words can undergo shifts in meaning over time due to cultural shifts or changes in societal norms. For instance, once neutral words might acquire positive or negative connotations.

Syntactic Changes: The way sentences are structured can also change. For example, word order might shift, or new constructions may emerge as old ones fade away.

Causes of Linguistic Evolution:

Several factors contribute to linguistic evolution:

Contact and Interaction: Language change often occurs through contact with other languages. This can happen through trade, conquest, colonization, or immigration, resulting in the borrowing of words, phrases, and grammatical structures.

Social and Cultural Influences: Changes in social norms, values, and cultural practices can lead to linguistic shifts. Language reflects societal attitudes, and as this changes, so does the way people express themselves.

Technological Advances: The introduction of new technologies can necessitate the creation of new terms to describe these advancements. This is particularly evident in fields such as computing and communication.

Generational Differences: Younger generations often introduce linguistic innovations, including changes in slang, pronunciation, and vocabulary. These innovations can eventually become widely accepted.

Language Evolution in Action:

One notable example of linguistic evolution is the transformation of Old English into Modern English. The Norman Conquest of England in 1066 brought about significant changes. The Normans spoke Old Norman, a language of Latin origin with Germanic influences. As a result of this conquest, English absorbed a substantial number of Norman French words, expanding its vocabulary and altering its phonology and grammar. This historical event illustrates how language change can be driven by political and social shifts. Similarly, the Internet and digital communication have played a substantial role in shaping the evolution of language in recent decades. The need to communicate quickly and concisely has led to the creation of new abbreviations, acronyms, and slang terms that are specific to online platforms and texting. The phrase "LOL," for example, has transitioned from a simple acronym for "laugh out loud" to a versatile expression of amusement or agreement.

Studying Linguistic Evolution:

Linguists and language historians study linguistic evolution to understand the mechanisms and patterns of language change, as well as the social, cultural, and historical contexts in which these changes occur. Comparative linguistics involves examining different languages, tracing their historical development, and identifying shared ancestral languages. The study of historical linguistics allows researchers to reconstruct the phonological, grammatical, and lexical features of past languages and to track how they evolved into their modern forms.

The Role of Language Preservation:

While linguistic evolution is a natural and ongoing process, there is also a need to preserve languages as cultural artifacts and tools for communication. Many languages are endangered due to factors such as globalization, language shift, and the dominance of major languages in education and media. Linguists work to document endangered languages and revitalize them through language revitalization programs and initiatives.

In conclusion, linguistic evolution is a complex and dynamic process that results from a variety of social, cultural, technological, and generational influences. Just as species evolve to adapt to changing environments, languages evolve to suit the ever-changing needs and contexts of their speakers. By studying linguistic evolution, linguists gain valuable insights into the historical, social, and cultural factors that shape language change. This understanding not only helps us appreciate the rich tapestry of languages that exist but also offers a window into the fascinating interplay between language and human society.

Chapter 3
Language Diversity and English Proficiency in the United States

While a record 64.7 million people ages 5 and older in the United States spoke a language other than English at home in 2015, a growing share of them are also fully proficient in English. Sixty percent of those speaking a foreign language at home were fully proficient in English in 2015, up from 56 percent in 1980—even as immigration levels rose significantly.

The population of immigrants and U.S. natives speaking a language other than English at home—which represents about one in five U.S. residents—has nearly tripled since 1980 when it stood at 23.1 million. This growth is not surprising: The immigrant population in the United States increased by 29.2 million people between 1980 and 2015, the lion's share coming from countries where English is not an official language. While immigrants learn English in school and in the workplace, their U.S.-born children grow up learning English while also hearing and speaking Spanish, Chinese, Vietnamese, Russian, and a host of other languages. Indeed, the U.S. Census Bureau records the use of more than 350 languages.

Just a few languages, however, account for the largest share of those spoken at home, with speakers of Spanish, Chinese, and Tagalog representing 70 percent of the overall population of immigrants and U.S. natives using a language other than English in the household. Most of these people are also fluent in English: The share of people who are bilingual (i.e., those who speak another language at home and reported that they speak English "very well") is more than half for the speakers of German, French, Tagalog, Arabic, Spanish, French Creole, and Russian (see Table 1).

Table 1. Top Ten Languages Other Than English Spoken in U.S. Homes, 2015

Rank	Languages Spoken at Home	Total	Bilingual Share (%)	LEP Share (%)
	Total	64,716,000	60.0	40.0
1	Spanish or Spanish Creole	40,046,000	59.0	41.0
2	Chinese	3,334,000	44.3	55.7
3	Tagalog	1,737,000	67.6	32.4
4	Vietnamese	1,468,000	41.1	58.9
5	French	1,266,000	79.9	20.1
6	Arabic	1,157,000	62.8	37.2
7	Korean	1,109,000	46.8	53.2
8	German	933,000	85.1	14.9
9	Russian	905,000	56.0	44.0
10	French Creole	863,000	58.8	41.2

Notes: Chinese includes Chinese, Mandarin, and Cantonese; French includes Patois and Cajun; German includes Pennsylvania Dutch.
Source: Migration Policy Institute (MPI) tabulation of data from the U.S. Census Bureau 2015 American Community Survey (ACS).

https://www.migrationpolicy.org/article/language-diversity-and-english-proficiency-united-states

The subset of this population that is Limited English Proficient (LEP) has fallen: 40 percent in 2015, compared to 44 percent in 1980. Limited English proficiency refers to anyone age 5 or older who reported speaking English less than "very well," as classified by the U.S. Census Bureau.

The U.S. Census Bureau assesses English language proficiency among residents who speak a language other than English at home by asking respondents to self-rate their English-speaking ability. The options given for this self-assessment are "very well," "well," "not well," or "not at all." This method is utilized to gather data on the linguistic diversity within the United States and to understand the level of English proficiency across different communities. The information collected is crucial for planning government programs for individuals who do not speak English well, ensuring the accessibility of public health information, legal regulations, voting materials, and safety guidelines in languages understood by the community members. It also plays a role in educational planning, helping schools understand the needs of their students and qualify for grants aimed at supporting students with limited English proficiency.

In 2015, more than 25.9 million people were LEP, accounting for 9 percent of the overall U.S. population ages 5 and older. While this number is high compared to earlier decades, the LEP population has been largely stable for the past five years (see Figure 1). In contrast, the overall number of foreign-language speakers has continued to rise since 2010, increasing linguistic diversity in the United States, albeit with the numbers not rising as fast as before. Although most of the LEP population in 2015 was foreign born, 18 percent of those speaking English less than "very well" were born in the United States.

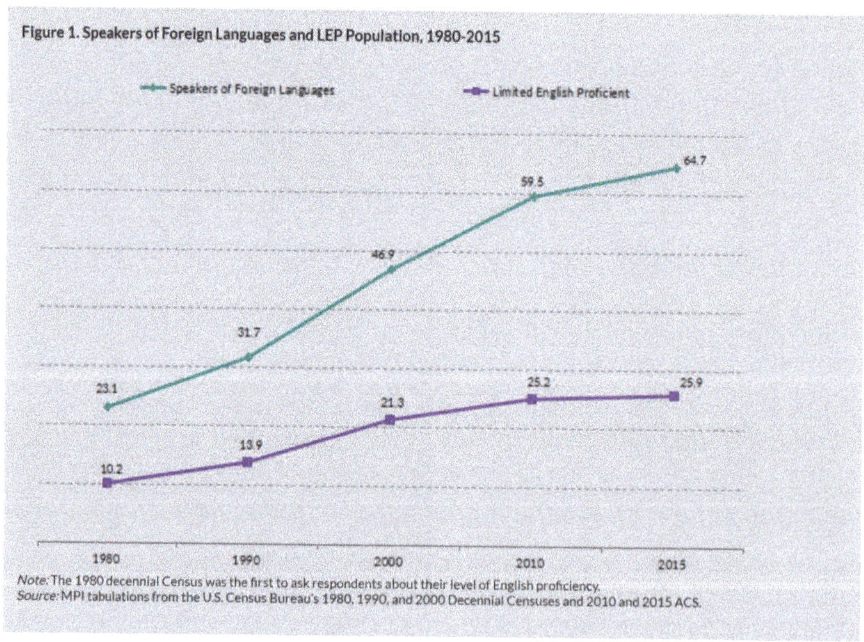

https://www.migrationpolicy.org/article/language-diversity-and-english-proficiency-united-states

Paarth Mathur

Immigrants to the United States come from many language backgrounds and while some speak English very well, roughly half of the total immigrant population of 43.3 million in 2015 was LEP.

The Limited English Proficient Population

Compared to the English-proficient population, the overall LEP population (immigrant and U.S. born) was less educated and more likely to live in poverty in 2015. Employed LEP men were much more likely to work in construction, natural resources, and maintenance occupations than English-proficient men, while LEP women were more than twice as likely to be employed in service and personal-care occupations than English-proficient women.

Using data from the U.S. Census Bureau (the most recent 2015 American Community Survey [ACS], 2010 ACS, and the 1980, 1990, and 2000 Decennial Census), this section of the Spotlight provides a demographic and socioeconomic profile of LEP individuals (ages 5 and older) residing in the United States, focusing on its size, geographic distribution, and socioeconomic characteristics.

Distribution by State and Key Cities

As of 2015, the highest concentrations of LEP individuals were found in the six traditional immigrant-destination states—California (6.8 million, or 26 percent of the total LEP population), Texas (3.6 million, 14 percent), New York (2.5 million, 10 percent), Florida (2.3 million, 9 percent), Illinois (1.1 million, 4 percent), and New Jersey (1 million, 4 percent). Together, the top six states accounted for approximately two-thirds of the 25.9 million LEP individuals.

Seven states had a higher share of LEP residents than the nationwide proportion of 9 percent. California had the highest share, with individuals reporting limited English proficiency accounting for 19 percent of the state population, followed by Texas and New York (14 percent each) (see Figure 2)

Voices: Linguistic and Cultural Dynamics of Refugee Population in America

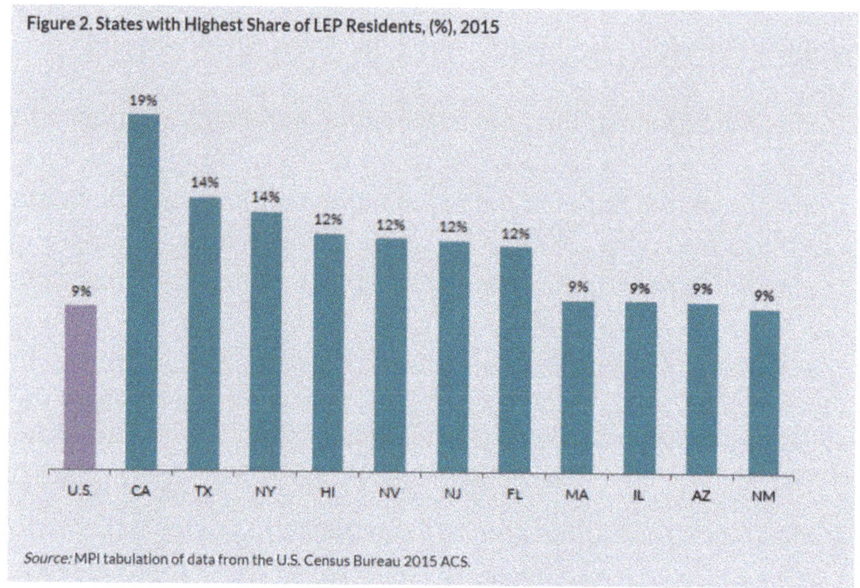

https://www.migrationpolicy.org/article/language-diversity-and-english-proficiency-united-states

In the 2010-2014 period, the top five counties with the largest LEP populations were Los Angeles County in California (9 percent of the U.S. LEP population), Miami-Dade County in Florida (3 percent), Harris County in Texas (3 percent), Cook County in Illinois (3 percent), and Queens County in New York (2 percent). Together, these five counties represented 21 percent of the total LEP population in the United States.

LEP residents accounted for more than one-third of the total population ages 5 and older in nine counties. Of these counties, seven were located in Texas, one in Alaska, and one in Florida. The counties with the highest share of LEP residents included Starr County, Texas (51 percent of the total county population, or 28,000 LEP residents); Maverick County, Texas (46 percent, 23,000); Webb County, Texas (44 percent, 103,000); Zapata County, Texas (42 percent, 5,000); and

Aleutians East Borough, Alaska (42 percent, 1,000). While most of these areas did not have large populations of LEP individuals in absolute terms relative to other counties, the share with limited English proficiency was significantly higher.

As of 2010-14, two metropolitan areas were home to 3 million or more LEP individuals: the greater New York (12 percent of the total U.S. LEP population) and Los Angeles (11 percent) metropolitan areas. The next three cities, with about 1 million LEP residents each, were the greater Miami (5 percent), Chicago (4 percent), and Houston (4 percent) metropolitan areas. Together, these five cities represented 37 percent of the U.S. LEP population.

LEP residents represented more than one-quarter of the total population ages 5 and older in six metropolitan areas, including four in Texas and two in California. The metropolitan areas with the highest share of LEP residents included Laredo, Texas (44 percent of total population, or 103,000 individuals); El Centro, California (33 percent, 53,000); McAllen, Texas (32 percent, 232,000); and El Paso, Texas (31 percent, 236,000).

Nativity

Whereas a majority of LEP individuals were foreign born in 2015, about 18 percent (4.7 million) **were** native born (see Figure 3).

Voices: Linguistic and Cultural Dynamics of Refugee Population in America

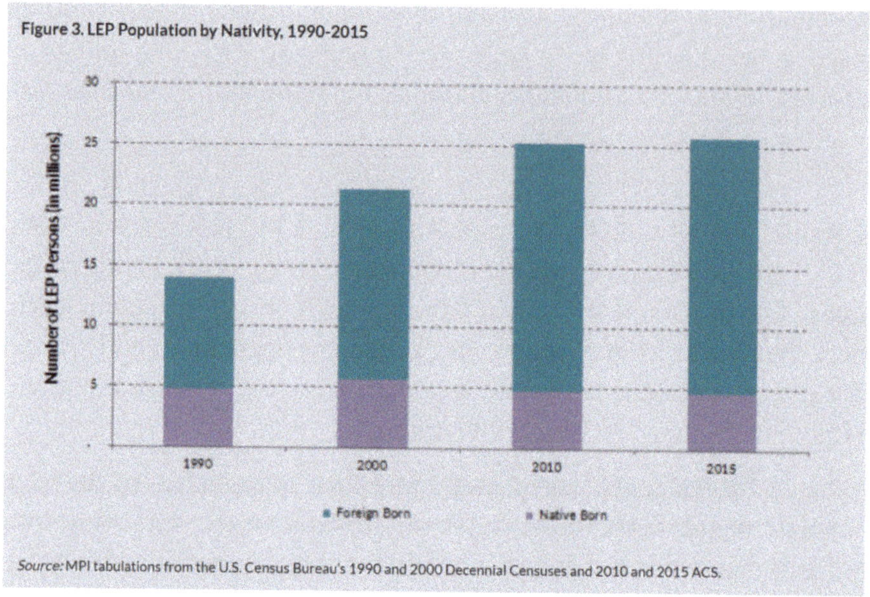

https://www.migrationpolicy.org/article/language-diversity-and-english-proficiency-united-states

The foreign-born population was much more likely to have limited English proficiency than the U.S.-born population (see Table 2). In 2015, approximately 49 percent of immigrants (21 million) were LEP, compared to 2 percent of the U.S.-born population.

Table 2. LEP Individuals (ages 5 and Older) in the United States by Nativity, 2015

	Total	LEP Population	LEP Share of Total Population (%)	Share of All LEP Individuals (%)
Native Born	258,794,000	4,707,000	1.8	18.3
Foreign Born	42,892,000	21,034,000	49.0	81.7
Total Population	**301,686,000**	**25,740,000**	8.5	100.0

Source: MPI tabulation of data from the U.S. Census Bureau 2015 ACS.

Paarth Mathur

Of the total foreign-born LEP population of 21 million, 38 percent were born in Mexico, followed by China/Hong Kong (7 percent), El Salvador (5 percent), and Vietnam and Cuba (4 percent each). The next five countries were the Dominican Republic, Guatemala, the Philippines, India, and Korea, with 3 percent each. Foreign-born LEP individuals were less likely than the overall immigrant population to be naturalized citizens (37 percent versus 48 percent, respectively).

Of the 4.7 million native-born LEP individuals, 14 percent were born in Puerto Rico and less than 2 percent were born in Mexico to at least one U.S.-citizen parent. Another 3 percent were born abroad elsewhere to at least one U.S.-citizen parent. Among the U.S. states, California and Texas were the birthplace of the highest share of native-born LEP persons, with about 19 percent each, followed by New York with about 7 percent.

Language Diversity

Spanish was the predominant language spoken by both immigrant and U.S.-born LEP individuals. About 64 percent (16.4 million) of the total LEP population spoke Spanish, followed by Chinese (1.8 million, or 7 percent), Vietnamese (867,000, 3 percent), Korean (592,000, 2 percent), and Tagalog (566,000, 2 percent). Close to 80 percent of the LEP population spoke one of these five languages.

There were marked differences, however, in the top languages spoken by LEP persons by nativity. Of the U.S.-born LEP population, 77 percent (3.6 million) spoke Spanish, followed by German (142,000, or 3 percent), Chinese (130,000, 3 percent), French (80,000, 2 percent), and Vietnamese (66,000, 1 percent). Among immigrant LEP individuals, Spanish was also the predominant language, spoken by about 61 percent (12.8 million). However, Asian languages were more likely to be spoken by the foreign-born LEP population, including Chinese (1.7 million, or 8 percent), Vietnamese (801,000, 4 percent), Korean (554,000, 3 percent), and Tagalog (531,000, 3 percent) (see Figure 4).

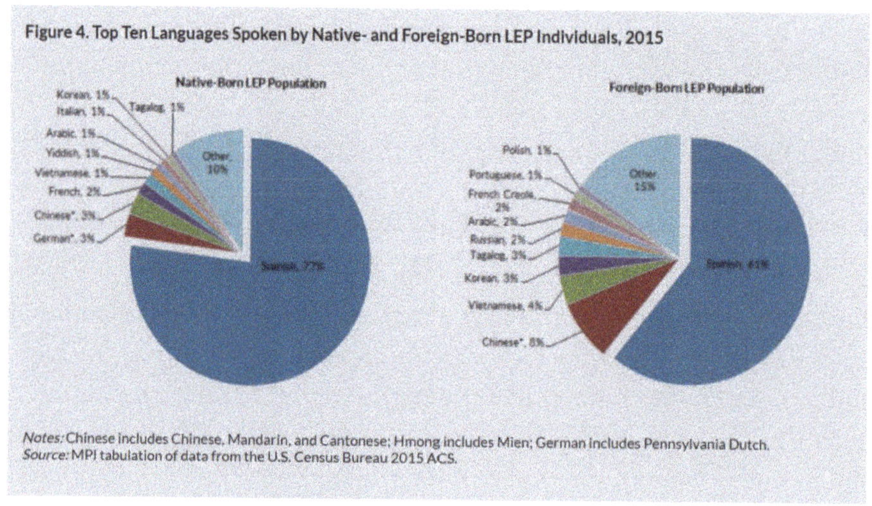

Notes: Chinese includes Chinese, Mandarin, and Cantonese; Hmong includes Mien; German includes Pennsylvania Dutch.
Source: MPI tabulation of data from the U.S. Census Bureau 2015 ACS.

https://www.migrationpolicy.org/article/language-diversity-and-english-proficiency-united-states

The linguistic diversity of the LEP population varied across the nation due to differing immigration trends and population composition. For instance, in 2015, the top three languages spoken by LEP residents in New York were Spanish, Chinese, and Russian. In contrast, the top three in Maine were French, Spanish, and Cushite. In Hawaii, Illocano, Tagalog, and Chinese were the top three languages spoken by LEP persons.

In addition, the LEP share among speakers of particular languages (including foreign- and native-born) varied widely. Burmese speakers had the highest share of limited English proficiency

(74 percent), compared to 58 percent of Vietnamese and Nepali speakers, and 55 percent of Chinese speakers. LEP individuals accounted for 41 percent of Spanish speakers.

Age, Race, and Ethnicity

Compared to their English-proficient counterparts, LEP individuals were much less likely to be of school age and much more likely to be of working age (see Table 3). In 2015, 9 percent of LEP individuals were children between the ages 5 and 17, versus 19 percent of the English-proficient population. Seventy-five percent were between ages 18 and 64 compared to 66 percent of English-proficient individuals. About 16 percent of both the LEP and English-proficient populations were senior citizens.

Table 3. Age Distribution by English Proficiency, 2015

Age Group	Limited English Proficient Share (%)	English Proficent Share (%)
Total	25,740,000	275,945,000
5 to 17	9.2	18.6
18 to 64	74.6	65.6
65 and over	16.2	15.8

Source: MPI tabulation of data from the U.S. Census Bureau 2015 ACS.

https://www.migrationpolicy.org/article/language-diversity-and-english-proficiency-united-states

LEP individuals were much more likely to be Latino or Asian than their English-proficient counterparts (see Figure 5). While Latinos comprised 62 percent of the LEP population, they accounted for 13 percent of the English-proficient population. Likewise, 22 percent of LEP individuals were Asian compared to 5 percent of English-proficient individuals.

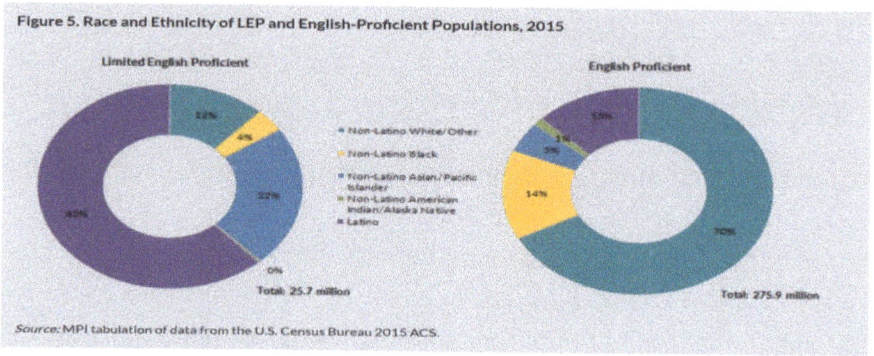

https://www.migrationpolicy.org/article/language-diversity-and-english-proficiency-united-states

Education and Employment

In general, LEP adults were much less educated than their English-proficient peers. As of 2015, 45 percent of all LEP individuals ages 25 and older lacked a high school diploma compared to 9 percent of their English-proficient counterparts. About 15 percent of LEP adults had a bachelor's degree or higher, compared to 32 percent of English-proficient adults.

LEP individuals ages 16 and older participated in the civilian labor force at a slightly lower rate than English-proficient individuals (60 percent versus 63 percent), largely because of greater gender differences in employment outcomes within the LEP population. Among English-proficient individuals, men participated in the civilian labor force at a higher rate than women (68 percent versus 59 percent), while the gender gap was much larger for LEP individuals (74 percent versus 48 percent).

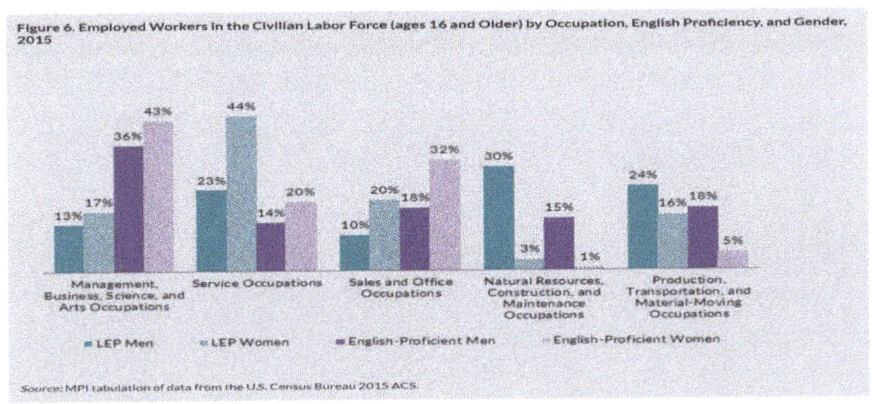

https://www.migrationpolicy.org/article/language-diversity-and-english-proficiency-united-states

Compared to their English-proficient counterparts, LEP men were more likely to work in natural resources, construction, and maintenance occupations (15 percent versus 30 percent), service occupations (14 percent versus 23 percent), and production, transportation, and material-moving occupations (18 percent versus 24 percent) (see Figure 6). LEP women were significantly more likely to work in service occupations (44 percent versus 20 percent), as well as production, transportation, and material-moving occupations (16 percent versus 5 percent) than their English-proficient counterparts.

Poverty

LEP individuals were more likely to live in poverty than English-proficient individuals. In 2015, about 23 percent of LEP individuals lived in households with an annual income below the official federal poverty line—nearly twice as high as the share of English-proficient persons (13 percent).

Community networks play a crucial role in the linguistic landscape of refugee populations. Community centers, cultural organizations, and religious institutions often provide spaces for

Voices: Linguistic and Cultural Dynamics of Refugee Population in America

language maintenance and cultural exchange. Additionally, technology and social media have emerged as critical tools for language learning and for maintaining connections with both the host society and diaspora communities worldwide.

The linguistic landscape of refugee populations has significant implications for policy, particularly in the areas of education, integration, and multiculturalism. Policies that support language learning, recognize the value of multilingual education, and celebrate linguistic diversity can contribute to more inclusive and cohesive societies. Moreover, access to translation and interpretation services in public services is crucial to ensure that refugees can navigate their new environments effectively.

The language dynamics within refugee communities vividly encapsulate the hurdles and complex situations these groups encounter as they adjust to new sociocultural settings. Marked by a rich diversity, continual evolution, and the capacity for adaptation, this linguistic scenario mirrors larger stories of movement, self-identity, and endurance. It highlights the significant role language plays in refugee experiences, from overcoming communication obstacles to seizing chances for cultural enrichment and forging community ties. Acknowledging and addressing the language requirements and assets of refugees is crucial for developing welcoming societies that honor and value diversity.

Migrants and
Refugees are not
pawns on the chess
board of humanity.

Chapter 4
The Language of the Unspoken
American Sign Language

Summary and Reflection on Personal Stories: The Impact of Sign Language and Non-Verbal Support in Refugee Integration

Migration plays a crucial role in the preservation and evolution of languages. Diaspora communities often become custodians of their native languages, passing them down through generations as a connection to their ancestral roots. At the same time, these languages evolve, blending with others and incorporating new influences to create dynamic, living dialects that reflect the hybrid identities of their speakers. For instance, the emergence of Spanglish in the United States or Hinglish in the United Kingdom highlights how languages morph and adapt in multicultural contexts.

In a world characterized by diverse cultures and languages, sign languages stand as unique and vibrant forms of communication for millions of individuals worldwide. With an estimated 300 different sign languages across the globe, these visual-spatial languages are the lifeblood of deaf communities, providing a means to express thoughts, emotions, and ideas. This article aims to shed light on the fascinating diversity of sign languages and explore their significance in fostering inclusion and cultural identity.

A Multifaceted Linguistic Landscape:

Sign languages are complete, natural languages, with their own grammatical rules, syntax, and vocabulary. Unlike spoken languages, which utilize sound, sign languages employ a rich array of handshapes, facial expressions, body movements, and spatial cues to convey meaning. These languages can be used for everyday conversations, storytelling, academic pursuits, artistic expression, and cultural preservation.

Global Distribution of Sign Languages:

Sign languages are not universal; they are regionally and culturally specific. Just as spoken languages have dialects and variations, sign languages exhibit distinct characteristics across different countries and even within specific regions. The estimated 300 sign languages span all continents, reflecting the diversity of the deaf communities they serve.

Examples of Sign Languages:

American Sign Language (ASL): ASL is one of the most widely recognized sign languages globally, predominantly used in the United States and parts of Canada. ASL has its own grammar and vocabulary, independent of English.

British Sign Language (BSL): BSL is the primary sign language in the United Kingdom and is distinct from ASL. It has its roots in French Sign Language (LSF) and developed alongside the British deaf community.

In deaf communities, people wave both hands in the air instead of clapping. Clapping can be disruptive and even painful for those who are hard of hearing or deaf. Waving is a way to show enthusiasm without being too loud. Clapping is primarily intended to create "sound" and is considered to belong to and/or show affiliation with "the Hearing world".

An interesting version of applause that we often see in the Deaf World is "clapping of the hands held overhead." Such an approach works well for mixed (Hearing and Deaf) performing troupes. Deaf people are able to see the clapping and the Hearing are able to both see and hear the clapping.

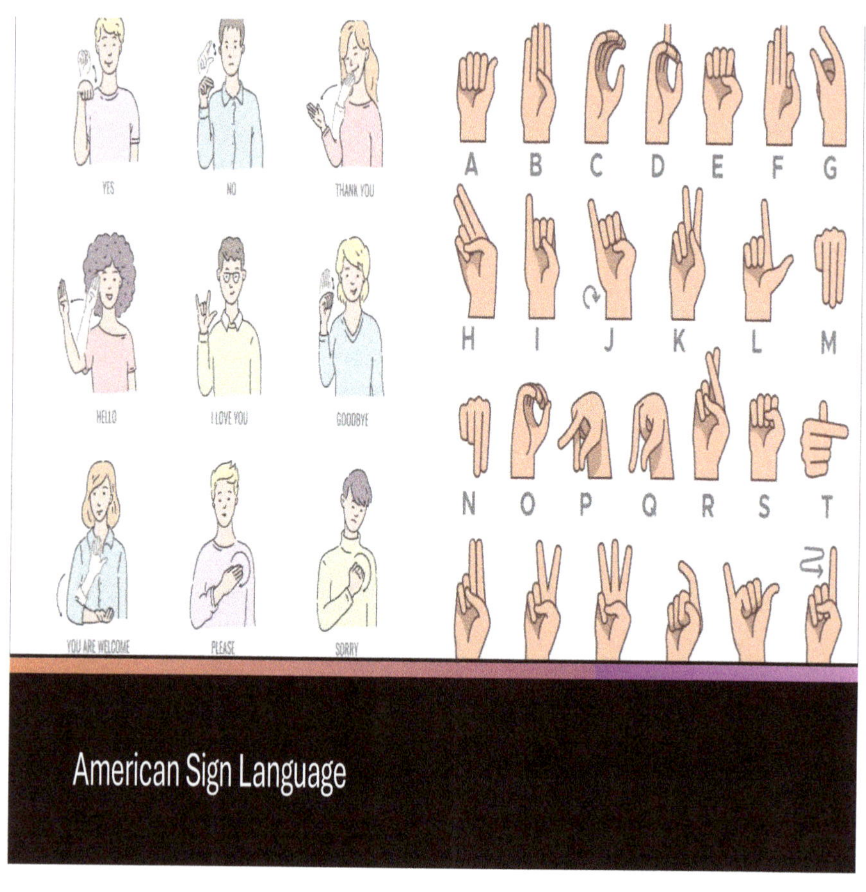

Australian Sign Language (Auslan): Auslan is used by the deaf community in Australia. Like other sign languages, Auslan evolved organically and has its own unique linguistic features.

Japanese Sign Language (JSL): JSL has a long history and differs significantly from spoken Japanese. It has its grammatical structures and is used by the deaf community in Japan.

Paarth Mathur

French Sign Language (LSF): known as Langue des Signes Française, is the sign language used by the deaf community in France. It is a complete and independent visual language that has evolved over centuries as a means of communication for individuals who are deaf or hard of hearing.

In deaf communities, people wave both hands in the air instead of clapping. Clapping can be disruptive and even painful for those who are hard of hearing or deaf. Waving is a way to show enthusiasm without being too loud. Clapping is primarily intended to create "sound" and is considered to belong to and/or show affiliation with "the Hearing world".

An interesting version of applause that we often see in the Deaf World is "clapping of the hands held overhead." Such an approach works well for mixed (Hearing and Deaf) performing troupes. Deaf people can see the clapping and the Hearing are able to both see and hear the clapping. LSF has its own grammar,

vocabulary, and syntax, distinct from spoken French. It incorporates a combination of handshapes, facial expressions, body movements, and spatial references to convey meaning. Like other sign languages, LSF is a rich and expressive mode of communication, capable of conveying nuanced concepts and emotions.

Indian sign language (ISL): ISL is the main sign language used in India by anywhere between 1 million to 2.7 million people, most of them Hearing Impaired (HI). The number of certified interpreters of ISL, however, is in the low hundreds, indicating an acute shortage as compared to the HI population.

ISL is used in the deaf community all over India. But ISL is not used in deaf schools to teach deaf children. Teacher training programs do not orient teachers towards teaching methods that use ISL. There is no teaching material that incorporates sign language.

Cultural Identity and Sign Languages: Sign languages are deeply intertwined with the cultural identity of deaf communities.

Voices: Linguistic and Cultural Dynamics of Refugee Population in America

They play a crucial role in fostering a sense of belonging, enabling cultural preservation, and providing a platform for artistic expression. Sign languages facilitate the transmission of folklore, storytelling, and historical narratives, allowing deaf individuals to connect with their heritage and celebrate their unique identity.

Despite their linguistic richness, sign languages have faced historical marginalization and limited recognition. Many countries have been slow to acknowledge sign languages as official languages or provide adequate resources for their education and preservation. However, progress is being made, with the United Nations recognizing the rights of deaf individuals and urging member states to support sign languages and deaf culture.

Recognizing the importance of sign languages in ensuring equal participation and access for deaf individuals, efforts are being made to promote their recognition and accessibility. Technology plays a vital role in facilitating communication between sign language users and non-signers, such as through video relay services and sign language translation apps. Education systems are gradually incorporating sign language as a subject, creating a more inclusive learning environment.

The vast array of sign languages worldwide is a testament to the linguistic and cultural diversity of deaf communities. Each sign language represents a unique expression of identity and provides a powerful means of communication and connection within its respective community. As we continue to strive for a more inclusive and accessible world, recognizing and supporting sign languages will be essential in fostering equality, diversity, and cultural understanding.

Paarth Mathur

Refugee crises:
A journey of Understanding

Many people around the globe have been internationally displaced due to refugee crises making it unsafe in their home country. From war with neighboring countries to internal gang violence and even religious persecution, there are many reasons why people leave their country in search of a better, safer life. In this chapter, I would like to highlight some of these stories and shed more light on the experiences of refugees.

The first story is of Alia, a girl from Syria who had to flee her home country to Lebanon. The crisis occurring in Syria is because of an internal rebellion against an oppressive government, who began killing people resisting their authoritarian regime to set an example. According to Alia," The roads were full of dead corpses. I saw dead people with no heads or no hands or legs. I was so shocked I couldn't stop crying."

Alia's horrifying story is one not uncommon among Syrian refugees forced to seek asylum in neighboring countries. Luckily, her life is much better in Lebanon, but the mass death and forced migration is a travesty that cannot be overstated.

Another story by Mapenzi Kangie tells of her experience being born in a refugee camp in Tanzania and growing up unable to go back to her true home. According to her, she "felt like I[she] was trapped. Trees surrounded me with nothing else to see; isolation made me feel hopeless. Seeing older people in the refugee camp left me wondering if I would be just like them, stuck in Nyarugusu my entire life."

Growing up in a refugee camp is a very dehumanizing experience, as it creates an almost prison for the people in them, unable to leave and experience life due to high chance of death. In favor of saving her life, Mapenzi never got to experience it until much later.

Voices: Linguistic and Cultural Dynamics of Refugee Population in America

Thankfully, her experience wasn't completely terrible. She was able to create a sense of community in that refugee camp, a sense of community that has carried her far and helped in making new friends and joining the international organization of migration.

Another story is from Roderick. He had to leave his home country of Zimbabwe due to political corruption and violence from his government, a common theme among Zimbabwe emigrants and a major contributor to its refugee crisis. He was able to immigrate to Australia and was easily able to acclimate into living in a free country. In his words," It sort of clicked. It was different to be in a country where you are free; free to move around, to talk… It was my first time in a free country." Today, he works as a firefighter and assisted in the numerous wildfires Australia experienced earlier this decade. His story is an inspiring reminder of the power of hard work and hope.

With all these refugee crisis, one thing remains clear, real change needs to be done to bring these issues to light and for involvement to be made in order to assist with them. In the remaining parts of this chapter, I will highlight some of these crises and explore why they happened.

Afghanistan: The removal of international troops from Afghanistan has led to the Taliban taking full political and economic control of the country, leading to periods of economic decline and political collapse. Mass carnage runs the streets of Afghanistan and the Darsi people.

Syria: Syria is undergoing a massive civil war, where the democratic rebel groups are resisting the government's authoritarian design. It began in small skirmishes at protests, but eventually developed into a full-blown civil war. While rebel forces have received support from NATO and GCC states, Russia's military intervention supporting the government led to the elimination of most of the rebel forces, causing a country overrun by corruption and no democracy.

South Sudan: South Sudan, like Syria, is also undergoing a civil war. In this case, the president of South Sudan, Salva Kiir, accused his former deputy of conspiring against him, causing his former deputy, Riek Machar, to start the Sudan's People Liberation Movement-in-Opposition. This led to a civil war. Ugandan troops deployed in support of the South Sudanese government, while the UN has not taken a side, and instead deployed peacekeepers as a part of the United Nations mission in Sudan. In January 2014, a ceasefire was reached, but after another conflict broke out, and a peace agreement signed in 2015, it took until 2020 for the fighting to stop, but, at that point, much of the damage to the country had been done.

Myanmar: The Myanmar refugee crisis is primarily fueled by one thing: the Rohingya genocide. The Rohingya genocide is a series of mass-killings of the Rohingya people, a primarily Muslim population, by the Myanmar government. The first phase of this genocide was a military crackdown occurring between October 2016 to January 2017, and the second phase has been occurring between August 2017.

A Baby Shower to remember.

In an increasingly interconnected world, understanding and celebrating cultural diversity is more important than ever. I recently had the privilege of organizing a baby shower for a group of refugee women in our community. This event was not just a celebration of impending motherhood but also an eye-opening journey into the rich tapestry of cultural diversity. Through this experience, I gained invaluable insights into the challenges, joys, and resilience of people from diverse backgrounds.

Voices: Linguistic and Cultural Dynamics of Refugee Population in America

The idea was born out of a desire to support and empower refugee women, who often face numerous challenges as they navigate their new lives in unfamiliar surroundings. Recognizing that pregnancy and motherhood are universal experiences that can transcend cultural and linguistic barriers, we saw an opportunity to bring together women from different backgrounds in a celebration that could foster community and support.

Planning the baby shower required careful consideration and cultural sensitivity. We collaborated with community leaders, online research and the women themselves to ensure that the event was respectful of their cultural norms and preferences. This collaboration was enlightening, as it exposed me to various cultural practices and traditions related to pregnancy and childbirth.

We decided on a neutral theme that celebrated new life, using decorations and symbols that were inclusive and representative of the various cultures of the participants. The menu was thoughtfully curated to include a variety of dishes that catered to different dietary restrictions and preferences, highlighting the importance of food in bringing people together.

The day of the baby shower was a beautiful tapestry of colors, languages, and traditions. As a cultural norm, I, being a male, was not allowed inside the room. I handled the check-in desk. As the women gathered, I was struck by the diversity in the room. There were women from Cuba, Turkey, and many other countries, each with their own stories of resilience and hope.

My coordinator told that later that each woman shared a tradition or custom related to motherhood from her culture. We heard about naming ceremonies from the respective countries, and the importance of community support in their culture. This event was not only educational but deeply moving, highlighting the commonalities and differences in our experiences of motherhood.

Organizing the baby shower for refugee women was an incredibly rewarding experience that taught me several key lessons about cultural diversity:

Empathy and Openness: Approaching cultural differences with empathy and an open mind is crucial for understanding and building connections with others.

Active Listening: Truly listening to the stories and experiences of people from diverse backgrounds can challenge and expand our perspectives.

Collaboration: Working together with individuals from different cultures can lead to richer, more inclusive outcomes.

Voices: Linguistic and Cultural Dynamics of Refugee Population in America

Resilience in Diversity: Despite the vast differences in our backgrounds, there is a shared strength and resilience that binds us, especially in the face of adversity.

The baby shower was more than just a celebration; it was a profound learning experience that underscored the beauty of cultural diversity and the universal bond of motherhood. It reminded me that while we may come from different parts of the world, our hopes, dreams, and aspirations for our children are remarkably similar. This event was a step towards building a more inclusive and supportive community, where diversity is not just acknowledged but celebrated. In doing so, it reinforced my belief in the power of coming together to support one another, irrespective of our backgrounds.

Transitioning from the exploration of the linguistic landscape, next chapter delves into the broader spectrum of cultural dynamics, offering a deeper understanding of the multifaceted experiences of refugee populations. Language serves as the bedrock upon which cultures are built and understood, and as we shift our focus from linguistic diversity to cultural dynamics, we uncover the intricate ways in which refugees navigate, negotiate, and transform their cultural identities within new sociocultural contexts. This transition underscores the profound interconnection between language and culture, highlighting how linguistic practices are enmeshed with cultural norms, values, and traditions. As we explore the cultural dynamics of refugee populations, we will examine the processes of cultural adaptation, the preservation of heritage, and the formation of new cultural syntheses, revealing the resilience and creativity of communities in flux. Through this examination, we aim to shed light on the complex tapestry of experiences that shape the identities and social fabric of displaced individuals and communities, ultimately enriching our understanding of human resilience and cultural exchange in the face of adversity.

Paarth Mathur

Chapter 5
Cultural Diversity:
America a Global Leader

Cultural Integration and Innovation: The immigrant experience is marked by a tension between the remembrance of their origins and navigating the complexities of a new society. Learning a new language, establishing oneself in unfamiliar surroundings, and adapting to a new community are among the numerous hurdles they encounter. Consequently, many immigrants find solace in the traditions and cultural practices of their homeland, such as religious customs, media, and festive celebrations that evoke a sense of familiarity.

However, the journey of immigrants is not solely anchored in the past. Many, especially the younger generation, draw inspiration from the opportunities available in American culture and the arts, exploring new forms of creative expression and blending their heritage with the new influences they encounter. This dynamic interplay between preserving their roots and embracing new possibilities enriches the cultural landscape of their new home.

Immigrants and their children are not born with more ability than anyone else. However, an immigrant (outsider) heritage may offer certain creative advantages to the miniscule fraction of persons possessing extraordinary talents. These advantages include: a resilience and determination to succeed, a curiosity and openness to innovation born of marginality, and an attraction to high-risk pursuits (because conventional careers are less open to them).

As an example, the welcoming attitude of the American arts and culture sectors towards individuals from diverse backgrounds can be attributed to several key factors. Firstly, the influx of a vast number of talented immigrants, some escaping adversity, and others in pursuit of new cultural experiences, was crucial. Equally significant was the swift expansion of the entertainment, culture, and science sectors, which prioritized individual talent over ancestry or social standing. This combination of factors helped create a vibrant and inclusive environment for creative expression and innovation.

Paarth Mathur

Frank Sinatra
The Son of Immigrants Who Revolutionized American Entertainment

Frank Sinatra, often hailed as one of the most influential and iconic American entertainers of the 20th century, made an indelible mark on the American entertainment industry through his contributions as a singer and actor. His story reflects the broader narrative of the American Dream, embodying the success that could be achieved by the children of immigrants in the United States. Frank Sinatra was born in Hoboken, New Jersey, in 1915, to Italian immigrants.

Sinatra's journey to stardom began in the swing era with Harry James and Tommy Dorsey, leading to his emergence as a solo artist who could captivate audiences with his voice and presence. With a career spanning several decades, Sinatra became renowned for his smooth, rich baritone and impeccable phrasing and timing, which allowed him to convey deep emotions in his music. His repertoire, featuring classics like "Fly Me to the Moon," "My Way," and "New York, New York," showcased his versatility across genres, including jazz, big band, and pop, influencing countless artists, and shaping the sound of American music.

Beyond his musical achievements, Sinatra's impact on the entertainment industry extended to his acting career. He won critical acclaim and an Academy Award for his role in "From Here to Eternity," demonstrating his prowess beyond the music stage. Sinatra's involvement in films added a new dimension to his legacy, blending his musical talents with his acting skills to create memorable performances that captivated moviegoers.

Sinatra's success story is deeply intertwined with the American cultural landscape of the 20th century. His rise to fame was not just a personal triumph but also a testament to the opportunities available in the United States for those with talent and determination, regardless of their background. This narrative played a significant role in the entertainment industry, highlighting the potential for immigrants and their descendants to achieve greatness and contribute to the cultural richness of the country.

Moreover, Sinatra used his influence for philanthropic efforts and civil rights advocacy, leveraging his status to support various causes and speak out against injustice. His actions reflected the ideals of inclusivity and equality, further enriching his legacy as a figure who not only entertained but also inspired and made a difference beyond the entertainment sphere.

The American entertainment industry, and indeed the country itself, benefited immensely from Sinatra's contributions. His music and films have left a legacy, continuing to inspire new generations of artists and entertainers. Sinatra's life and career exemplify how the son of immigrants could become an emblematic figure of American culture, embodying the values of hard work, talent, and the pursuit of excellence.

Frank Sinatra's story is a vivid illustration of the American Dream realized. His contributions to music and film have become an integral part of the country's cultural heritage, demonstrating the profound impact that individuals from diverse backgrounds can have on the American entertainment industry and society at large.

Despite their outsider status, immigrants may have benefited from their marginality. A biographer of William Wyler (who received a record twelve Academy Award nominations for film directing), observed that Wyler was fascinated with America and things American, and as a foreigner he saw things from the point of view of an interested and sympathetic outsider. Marginality is often considered to be a disadvantage. Migration, upward mobility, and intermarriage can bring people into new contexts where their mother tongue, religion, and cultural expectations are not the norm. The new experiences–cultural shock, feelings of loss, and uncertainty–are generally uncomfortable, at least until the new culture becomes familiar. Many immigrants, particularly those who arrive as adults, never really feel at home in the place of settlement.

However, marginality can also stimulate creativity. Bilingual persons have more than multiple words for the same object–they often have multiple interpretations and multiple subjectivities about emotions, responses, and relationships. Similarly, persons who have been socialized in two or more cultures have broader imaginations about the range of human responses to love, death, family, and other aspects of life. Marginality, combined with extraordinary talent and strong artistic sensitivity, leads to greater openness to innovation.

Generational Shifts in Tradition and Innovation: The transition from tradition to innovation is not merely a rejection of the past but a complex interplay between maintaining cultural roots and exploring new forms of expression. This dynamic is vividly illustrated in the entertainment industry, where immigrant performers and their descendants have played pivotal roles.

Economic Contributions: Beyond culture, immigrants have made substantial economic contributions. Despite facing initial challenges, their resilience, creativity, and entrepreneurial spirit have often led to significant advancements in various fields, including science, technology, and cuisine.

Social Impact: The integration of immigrants and refugees has not only enriched the American cultural landscape but also challenged and expanded the notion of American identity. By weaving their unique backgrounds into the fabric of American society, they have played a crucial role in shaping a more inclusive and diverse national identity.

Challenges and Opportunities: The journey of immigrants and refugees in America underscores a broader narrative of struggle, adaptation, and success. While they have faced significant challenges, their contributions highlight the potential of diversity as a source of strength and innovation.

Voices: Linguistic and Cultural Dynamics of Refugee Population in America

In conclusion, the integration of immigrants and refugees into American society has significantly contributed to the nation's cultural diversity and enhancement. Their stories of perseverance, innovation, and creativity underscore the value of embracing diversity as a pathway to a richer, more inclusive society.

Paarth Mathur

Is U.S. Falling Short of Refugees Expectations as a Global Leader

For the first time on record, the global number of people forced to flee their homes has crossed the staggering milestone of 100 million, according to recent data from UNHCR, the UN Refugee Agency.

That 100 million includes refugees, asylum seekers, and those displaced inside their borders by conflict. If they were a single country, it would be the 14th most-populous nation in the world. "It's a record that should never have been set," UN High Commissioner for Refugees Filippo Grandi said in a press statement. "This must serve as a wake-up call."It should especially serve as a wake-up call for rich countries like the United States that have fallen short of their moral and political responsibilities to the displaced.

"We very much have a national mythos around being a safe haven and being a nation of immigrants," said Elizabeth Foydel, the private sponsorship program director at the nonprofit International Refugee Assistance Project. "And for a long time, the US was the top country in terms of resettlement. But I think it's fair to say that we've been falling short over the past several years. You see a significant decline overall."

Just look at this chart. From a high in 1980, when the US Refugee Act was signed into law, the number of admitted refugees has generally declined.

Voices: Linguistic and Cultural Dynamics of Refugee Population in America

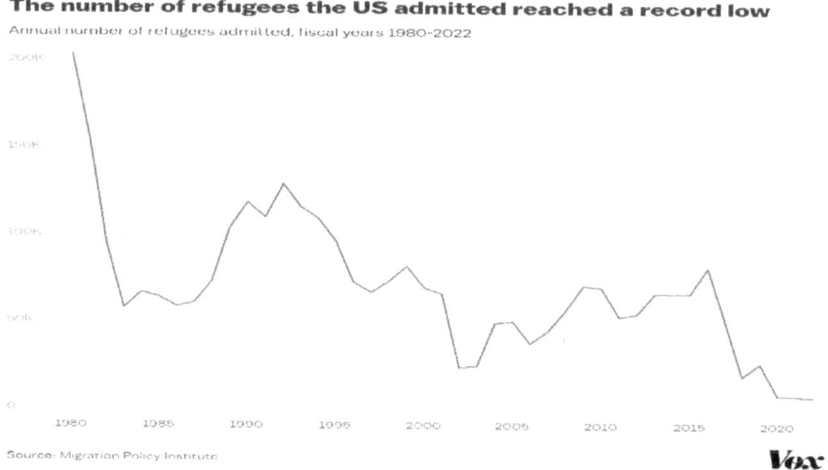

The data shows variations tied to global crises, with notable increases in refugee numbers following the Soviet Union's collapse in the 1990s and the intensification of the Syrian refugee crisis in 2016. Despite these peaks, there's a discernible decline over recent decades in refugee support from certain quarters, contrasting sharply with the rising trend of global displacement.

The US has the capacity, resources, and room to be a safe haven for many, many people. Yet the current reality is that other countries around the world — often countries that have far less capacity and fewer resources — are hosting far greater numbers of displaced people relative to their population than the US is. In fact, at least until the war in Ukraine, developing countries were hosting 85 percent of the world's refugees. According to the UN Refugee Agency, these five countries were hosting the most refugees as of mid-2021:

- Turkey: 3.7 million

- Colombia: 1.7 million

- Uganda: 1.5 million

- Pakistan: 1.4 million

- Germany: 1.2 million

To be clear, for a country to host a refugee does not necessarily mean it's going to permanently resettle that refugee. And to a degree, it's not surprising to find a lot of refugees in the countries neighboring their countries of origin. Some people may want to stay close to home in the hope that they can return, and getting from, say, Syria to Turkey is easier than getting all the way to the US.

Still, "many of these low- and middle-income countries don't have the resources to be able to care for their own population, let alone millions of newcomers," said Helen Dempster, an assistant director at the Center for Global Development. Yet developing countries have had to sustain millions of refugees for years because of insufficient resettlement from richer countries around the world, including the US. That, Dempster said, "leaves refugees with few options but to stay close to home."

Voices: Linguistic and Cultural Dynamics of Refugee Population in America

Foydel agrees. "The distribution of displaced people might look different if we actually had more robust resettlement by the US and other countries," she said.

So, why has refugee resettlement been declining in the US?

If you look back 40 years ago or so, you can see that refugee resettlement used to be a bipartisan issue. In recent years, there has been a noticeable increase in the politicization of aspects that are traditionally seen as fundamental to the American ethos.

The 9/11 attacks were a major inflection point. After that, it became more common to view refugees especially those from the Middle East as possible security threats. The resulting security vetting process became so incredibly rigorous as to function as a bottleneck.

Then came the rise in nativist discourse.

Nativist discourse refers to a form of dialogue or rhetoric that emphasizes the interests and culture of native-born inhabitants over those of immigrants. It often includes themes of protecting national identity, prioritizing the needs of the native population, and expressing concerns over the impact of immigration on social, economic, and cultural aspects of society. This discourse can sometimes lead to exclusionary policies and attitudes towards immigrants and refugees.

Since the funding of refugee agencies is tied to the refugee camp, agencies were forced to lay off staff and shutter offices. Canada — which has little more than a 10th of the US population overtook America as the global leader in resettlement.

The Covid-19 pandemic didn't help the matter either. Although it's understandable that Covid-19 shutdowns and travel restrictions hindered resettlement earlier in the pandemic, refugee advocates say that's no longer an excuse.

Chapter 6
Integration Barriers:
Perspectives from Refugee Youth

The voices of young refugees are pivotal in fostering cultural diversity and engagement. They bring unique perspectives, stories, and traditions that enrich the cultural tapestry of any society. Listening to and valuing these voices not only facilitates their integration and adjustment but also promotes mutual understanding and respect among diverse communities. Through sharing their experiences, young refugees can challenge stereotypes, inspire empathy, and encourage social cohesion. Their active participation in cultural dialogues contributes to a more inclusive and vibrant society, where diverse backgrounds are celebrated as strengths rather than seen as barriers. Engaging with young refugees thus plays a crucial role in building a dynamic, multicultural community.

Young refugees identify and discuss the major challenges they face while adapting to life in America, with cultural adaptation emerging as the primary concern. These obstacles, along with their causes, impacts, and possible solutions, were all highlighted by the refugee youth themselves. Please take a moment to understand the struggles young refugees encounter and think about ways you can help make their transition smoother.

Cultural adjustment is complicated for refugees. Adjusting to a new culture can be a difficult challenge for refugees to accept. If they do accept this new culture and begin to re-establish and find an identity it becomes challenging to keep everyone in both cultures happy. Yet, a lack of cultural adjustment limits communication, acceptance, and inclusion.

One of the main causes that makes cultural adjustment so difficult for refugees is that everything is different and new in the U.S. Refugees often come to the U.S. with idealistic expectations and reality can be disappointing. It is challenging to adapt to a new home, climate, and customs, and can make a person feel like they don't belong anywhere. Additionally, most young refugees' families do not want them to completely forget their native culture in order to fit into American society. It is challenging to find balance with new and old culture and this dichotomy makes it difficult to adjust to their new life. If they stay in their own community too much and don't get involved in their new town and school, it makes adjusting to the new culture almost impossible. Another factor that makes cultural adjustment a barrier for refugees, is that some Americans do not want to let refugees into their culture and world. Media stories influence and enforce stereotypes of refugees.

Struggling with cultural adjustment can make refugees feel isolated, pressured, depressed, and intimidated. The intimidation and fear of this new culture can make them not want to participate in school, activities, and the community. If they do not adapt well, they are often discriminated against and bullied for being different. The peer pressure to fit in and adjust can make them change their values or beliefs and participate in risky behaviors. For some, it means deculturation and completely trading their native culture for American culture because they can't find a balance. In turn, if they are accepted into this new culture, they might be considered a traitor in their native culture, which leads to family conflict and tension. Cultural adjustment can lead to a loss of identity. Refugee youth can become insecure and unstable and unsure of who they are. This leads to difficulty in decision making. It is difficult to know which way of living is the right one.

Schools can promote bi-culturalism and offer peer-to-peer cultural exchanges, like an American friend program.

Organizations that work in refugee camps can improve orientation prior to arrival so there is not as much culture shock upon arrival. Refugee resettlement agencies can give a more in-depth cultural orientation sessions or have one that is specifically geared towards refugee youth. They can try to help with inter-generational challenges that arise from adjusting and assimilating to a new culture. They can encourage refugees to get involved in the community as well as local cultural and ethnic community-based organizations so they can adjust to their new culture while practicing their native traditions.

The media can send positive messages about refugees and resettlement. American citizens can learn about different cultures and work on accepting these differences. Communities and towns can host inter-faith celebrations and have cultural festivals to encourage acceptance and integration.

Cultural Adaptation and Integration: A Phased Approach

Four stages can be discerned and are presented in a necessarily simplified form below. In practice, the process for individuals is not a linear one. Rather, most will move back and forward and there may be times when reactions lie somewhere between the stages. Integration support will be most important in the culture shock and adjustment stages. These are not only stressful points in the resettlement process but are stages at which intervention can help to ensure a positive outcome. The time involved in adjustment will differ depending on the characteristics of individual resettled refugees, their past experiences and factors in the resettlement environment.

Honeymoon Phase: The Honeymoon Phase often occurs soon after arrival to the intended destination and typically lasts for a few weeks to a few months. It may be characterized by feelings of curiosity, excitement, and relief.

Culture Shock Phase: In the Culture Shock Phase, feelings of excitement may give way to worry, frustration, anger, and homesickness. activities can seem difficult as the newcomer struggles to concentrate. The Culture Shock phase typically lasts months, but again is dependent on the individual and what they do to cope in the situation. Should an individual remain in the culture shock phase for an extended period, additional support, such as that offered by a counsellor may likely help.

Adjustment Phase: Generally, after 6 to 12 months, the newcomer enters the Adjustment Phase. In this phase, routines begin to develop, and new information becomes easier to process. The newcomers sense of humor returns, and they may find themselves more relaxed and confident.

Mastery Phase: In the Mastery Phase, the newcomer feels comfortable in their receiving community, although they will still experience periods of difficulty.

Adapting to American Culture: Immigrants adapting to new culture may worry about changes in customs and lifestyle, among other aspects of the new culture. However, taking the right approach and giving yourself plenty of time to adapt can help ease the transition to American culture.

Some small and specific tips for adapting to the culture in the U.S. may include:

Remaining Optimistic About the Transition: Moving to the U.S. as an immigrant comes with many changes, whether here on business or as a long-term resident. Immigrants will need to adapt to spending a long time away from friends and family, along with other aspects of their home country that might differ from their American destination. It can be challenging to adjust to this change, but it's all part of the process of starting a new and exciting life.

It may feel like a big change that individuals may be afraid to make, but the fact is that they will still be able to see their loved ones while starting a fresh new life in America. Many immigrants even wind up bringing their families to the U.S. once they've had a chance to establish themselves.

It's best to look at these changes as a positive thing, as immigrants can still be themselves as they navigate a new environment that can benefit them in many ways. Immigrants moving to the U.S. will have the chance to develop a career that makes them happy, a comfortable lifestyle, and healthy relationships that make the move worthwhile.

Taking the Time to Assimilate the Culture: It may require some patience and ample time, but it's important for Chicago immigrants to take steps to gradually integrate into the culture. This entails learning English and other languages that are commonly spoken in the U.S., along with getting used to local customs such as greetings and general interactions.

There are many ways to approach learning the language and local culture, from taking free online courses to practicing with people regularly. Immigrants should avoid closing themselves off and isolating, as this can only make it harder to integrate and take full advantage of what the culture has to offer.

Exploring Your Neighborhood: One way to absorb the American culture when new to the U.S. is to wander around your area. Depending on where you reside in the country, the subculture could be considerably different. For example, life on the east coast might be different from life on the west coast. Certain cities also have different cultures. Getting to know your area and its inhabitants can give you a better sense of what to expect in your neighborhood as you adapt to a new way of life.

Enjoy American Food: Another step you can take to get into the American culture is to try various American dishes. Visiting and ordering from local restaurants in your area can expose you to many new tastes and local flavors. The cuisine can also vary greatly from state to state and city to city, making it ideal to try different dishes that broaden your tastes.

Share Your Own Culture with Others As you connect with American citizens, don't shy from sharing your own experience. People around you may find your story fascinating and give them some insight into how you're adapting to American culture. Based on your unique experience, people may be more accommodating and eager to introduce you to different aspects of American culture. For instance, people may recommend specific places to visit to give you a better sense of American life, or they may suggest certain TV shows or films to further help with this.

Remembering That There Are Many Others Facing the Same Situation: Immigrants in the U.S. are far from alone. There are millions of immigrants in the U.S., with 22.5 million legally registered refugees who were forcibly uprooted from their home countries, according to data from the United Nations High Commissioner for Refugees (UNHCR). Whether in the U.S. voluntarily or out of hope for a brighter future as a refugee, immigrants share many of the same struggles and adjustments as they seek to integrate into American culture. It can help to remember that many fellow immigrants are experiencing a similar situation, which can add a sense of camaraderie as they settle into the U.S.

Avoiding Judging Others: Immigrants adapting to American culture may find the changes to be extreme, to the point where they may want to resist those changes. However, it's best to keep an open mind and avoid placing judgment on others. Understanding how others live and their culture can make it easier to transition without causing any loss of identity.

Knowing That it's Okay to Make Mistakes Along the Way: With so many differences between American culture and others, immigrants may make mistakes when it comes to communication and interactions, but this is expected with any new experience. For instance, some may have a way of greeting others in their home country that is considered unusual or incorrect in the U.S.

People are often forgiving and take these errors in good humor: Over time, mistakes will become less common until they're rarely made. Even if they're still made from time to time, people will likely overlook them.

Taking all these steps can help immigrants make the most of their move to the U.S. There are certain hardships that immigrants may fear, but by practicing diligence, open-mindedness, and patience, immigrants can have an easier time adjusting to what may seem to some like a very alien culture. With the right mindset and proper precautions, immigrants from all walks of life and locations across the globe can find a rewarding experience waiting for them in the U.S.

Voices: Linguistic and Cultural Dynamics of Refugee Population in America

Staying open to change is key to making the transition less challenging as they adapt to this new culture.

Paarth Mathur

Integration Challenges of Refugee Population

Linguistic integration refers to the process of individuals or groups adapting to and becoming proficient in a language that is not their mother tongue, within a community where that language is dominant. This process is crucial for social cohesion, education, and employment opportunities in multicultural and multilingual societies. However, it poses several challenges, both for the individuals undergoing integration and for the societies facilitating this process. Here's a summary of the main challenges:

Difficulty speaking and learning English: Let's be honest- my country, the United States, is not known for being multilingual. So, imagine arriving here, unable to speak English. Try getting a job, making friends, or even completing basic tasks like buying food or filling out forms. To address this, many refugees and immigrants take ESL classes, but finding the time between jobs and caring for kids can be difficult. Especially difficult if you weren't literate in your native tongue to begin with.

Raising children and helping them succeed in school: One of the biggest obstacles refugees and immigrant parents report is raising their children in a new, unfamiliar culture. Parents often find that their children are quickly "Americanized," which may be at odds with their own culture. Additionally, kids tend to pick up English much faster than their parents. This throws off the parent-child dynamic, and you know that kids, especially teens, are going to use this to their advantage.

Voices: Linguistic and Cultural Dynamics of Refugee Population in America

With regards to school, parents often feel disappointed to see their children struggling to keep up in class, and many parents report bullying and discrimination because of cultural differences. Kids are often placed by their age rather than by their ability, and for those who are unable to speak English, it's virtually impossible to keep up. To add further insult to injury, parents may not have the education or language skills to assist their children, and they may not be able to communicate with faculty to address the problem.

Securing work: While most refugees and immigrants are happy to take whatever job is available when they first enter the country, finding a job, and slowly moving up the ladder, is incredibly difficult. Even if you ignore undocumented immigrants who face additional challenges securing work, trouble speaking English is a major problem in positions you might not expect like labor. Refugees and immigrants who are educated and who formerly had strong jobs back home, find it frustrating that they can't obtain the same jobs here.

Employers typically prefer work experience within the US, and certifications outside of the US usually don't transfer. That's why it's not uncommon for your taxi driver to have formerly worked as an educator or engineer.

Additionally, refugees and immigrants are easy victims for discrimination and exploitation in the workplace. Some employers recognize the sense of urgency and desperation among these groups to keep their jobs, so they will have them take the less desirable and even dangerous roles. Undocumented immigrants, particularly, assume they have no rights, and workers who can't speak English are easy targets.

Securing housing: I don't have to tell you that safe, affordable housing is expensive. So, imagine trying to obtain that with low-paying jobs. For that reason, large families often choose to live together, creating stressful, noisy environments that are hardly conducive to studying or resting.

Again, refugees and immigrants fall victim to exploitation, this time from their landlords. In Utah, for instance, I worked with a group of Karen refugees from Myanmar who were forced to live in apartments known by the landlord to have bedbugs. Once, one of those buggers was spotted, the families would be forced to pay an expensive fee to have them removed, and the landlord would attempt to charge them additional fees or threaten to kick them out. Unable to speak English and unfamiliar with our laws, many of the families complied-even though it was clearly a scam.

Accessing services: Undocumented immigrants have an especially difficult time accessing services, largely because they are afraid of being deported. Consequently, people will avoid seeing the doctor or reaching out for services like legal guidance when they're badly needed.

Those who are here legally aren't necessarily in the clear, though. Difficulty speaking English, trouble taking off work, and limited transportation (we'll get to that) are all very real issues. Accessing mental health issues is especially problematic. Many times, refugees and immigrants have been exposed to violence, rape, even torture- but they may not know how to seek help. Furthermore, mental health issues are taboo in many cultures, creating an additional barrier for those in need.

For those who can successfully obtain the services they need, the experience is usually negative. In Utah, I heard stories about law enforcement professionals misunderstanding a victim's statement due to language barriers, and doctors misdiagnosing sick patients for the same reason.

Transportation: Like language barriers, trouble with transportation is an issue that affects nearly every aspect of life for refugees and immigrants.

Obtaining a driver's license, whether documented or not, is extremely difficult for a variety of reasons. For those who don't speak English, a translator is needed, and they aren't easy to come by. Also, the driver must be literate to pass the written exam.

With some luck, families will have one car to share among them, but getting kids to and from school, as well as getting adults to and from work can be challenging. Many times, the men will keep the car, leaving it up to the women to find their own rides from friends or coworkers. As you can imagine, having so many people rely on one car makes it incredibly difficult to fit in additional commitments like ESL classes and medical appointments.

But hey, what about public transportation? While many refugees and immigrants do rely on public transportation to get around, it can be incredibly frightening for some. In Utah, a man I worked with from the International Rescue Committee shared a story about one of his clients. The client was from a very rural town where there were no paved roads or traffic signs. My coworker recognized that because of her limited English, she might need assistance figuring out how to take the bus to reach the IRC for her appointments. He accompanied the woman to and from the IRC for her first appointment, but assumed she would be fine on her own from then on. The next week, he received a call from her, crying and terrified.

Because she was not familiar with our roads, she had never learned how to cross the street safely nor how to read the traffic signs. Consequently, several cars honked at her while she illegally crossed the street. She then got on the correct bus but became confused as to what stop she needed to get off at and was unable to ask. I can only imagine how scary that must have been for her.

Cultural barriers: Again, just like transportation and trouble speaking English, cultural barriers transcend each aspect of life for refugees and immigrants.

Here's an example. In Utah, a group of Latter-Day Saints were organizing a weeklong hike for youth in the desert. Some of the organizers thought it might be a nice idea to include some of the refugee youth, as a way in integrate them into the community and help them make friends with some of the local kids. I remember hearing about this and thinking it was such a wonderful idea. But, less than a day into the hike, some of the refugee kids became very upset. The hike, it turned out, had reminded them of the time when they were forced to flee their homes. Now, despite the group's kindest intentions, these kids were being retraumatized. This just goes to show how easy it is for these kinds of cultural misunderstandings to take place.

Despite all these challenges, the people I worked with were incredibly strong and grateful for the opportunity to be in the United States. Most of them had such basic desires: to have their children succeed in school and to be able to put a roof over their heads. After everything they had already been through, they were doing all that they could to keep their families afloat in this new, scary place.

Curious what you can do? It's simple! So many refugees and immigrants, particularly undocumented, feel like outsiders, or worse- they feel invisible. So, if you come across someone who can tell is new to the country, start a conversation! I'm guessing he or she will have some amazing stories to share.

Voices: Linguistic and Cultural Dynamics of Refugee Population in America

Funding for English Language Education Has Declined. although the outlook for linguistic integration is generally positive, the barriers to English proficiency particularly for immigrants who are low-skilled, poorly educated, residentially segregated or undocumented—are cause for concern.

Funding for English-as-a-second-language classes has declined even as the population of English language learners has grown. English language learners account for 9 percent of all children in the K-12 system—and this presents challenges for many school systems. Overall, resources for education in English as a second language are limited for both adults and children, which may present barriers to successful integration, particularly in the first generation.

Paarth Mathur

Chapter 7
Linguistic Challenges
Role of Policy and the Way Forward

The changing linguistic landscape calls for nuanced language policies that balance the need for a common lingua franca for integration and communication with the need to preserve and celebrate linguistic diversity. Educational systems play a crucial role in this regard, offering language support to newcomers while also incorporating multilingual education models that value all languages as assets.

Language learning and exchange programs can also foster mutual understanding and respect, breaking down barriers and building bridges between communities. Such initiatives not only facilitate integration but also enrich the linguistic repertoire of all participants, creating more vibrant and inclusive societies.

Educating refugees through "Citizenship Classes and Tests" presents a complex dynamic between integration and autonomy. While such educational initiatives aim at preparing refugees for successful integration into their new communities by familiarizing them with the legal, social, and cultural norms, they raise important questions. This approach can be seen as empowering, offering refugees the tools and knowledge for informed participation in their new society. Conversely, it could be perceived as coercive if participation is mandatory without accommodating the refugees' diverse backgrounds and needs. The effectiveness and ethical considerations hinge on the execution and flexibility of these programs to respect refugees' autonomy while aiding their integration.

To encourage linguistic diversity, policies should encompass multilingual education, where curriculums include instruction in minority languages alongside the dominant language. Government services and official documents should be available in multiple languages to ensure accessibility for all citizens. Additionally, supporting media in diverse languages and promoting cultural events that celebrate linguistic heritage can help preserve minority languages. Funding for research and documentation of lesser-known languages is also crucial for their preservation. These strategies collectively contribute to a society that values all languages as assets, fostering an environment of inclusion and cultural richness.

In the U.S. education system, languages taught vary widely but commonly include Spanish, French, Mandarin, German, and Italian, reflecting both global relevance and local demographic influences. The selection of languages offered is often determined by factors such as teacher availability, community interest, and the perceived importance of the language in global affairs. Additionally, schools might offer languages like Arabic, Japanese, and Russian, aiming to prepare students for a diverse and interconnected world. The focus is increasingly on not just learning to communicate but also understanding cultural contexts.

The U.S. education system incorporates languages spoken by refugees to varying degrees, depending on the diversity and policies of the local education agencies. While major languages like Spanish, Arabic, and Chinese see more structured integration into curricula and bilingual programs, lesser-known languages spoken by refugees might not be as prominently featured. Schools often respond to the linguistic needs of their refugee students through English as a Second Language (ESL) programs, while also attempting to support the maintenance of students' native languages as part of multicultural and inclusive education initiatives.

Paarth Mathur

Building Meaningful Refugee Participation into Protection Policymaking

Worldwide, there is a pressing need for more effective policies to address protection and displacement challenges. One promising but underutilized component of addressing this challenge is meaningfully engaging refugees themselves in policymaking processes to ensure their knowledge, expertise, and unique perspectives are reflected in program design and that they have a shared sense of ownership over implementation. While the protection community acknowledged this in the 2018 Global Compact on Refugees, there is a general dearth of evidence on how, concretely, refugee participation can foster better policies. Similarly, there have seemingly been limited efforts to develop clear theories of change that outline how refugee participation initiatives are supposed to achieve their goals and to document these initiatives' processes and outcomes. As participation efforts continue to emerge globally, stakeholders ranging from states and the United Nations High Commissioner for Refugees (UNHCR) to refugee-led organizations and networks have an opportunity to sharpen their understanding of the goals of refugee participation, how to best reach them, and how to remove barriers that impede progress. To make these links explicit and ground participation opportunities in best practices, robust evaluations and stronger evidence will be essential. One notable development in recent years has been a shift in the rationale behind refugee participation initiatives. While calls for meaningful participation have often relied on a moral argument (that displaced people should be involved in decisions that affect them), stakeholders are increasingly making the pragmatic case for this engagement as well: that refugee participation has the potential to improve the effectiveness of policies and programs at the design and implementation stages.

Voices: Linguistic and Cultural Dynamics of Refugee Population in America

84

At the design stage, engaging refugees can allow other stakeholders to tap into information that only refugees have access to, and it may reveal resources, networks, and solutions that policymakers were not aware of. As a result, the policies should align better with refugees' preferences and needs.

At the implementation stage, refugees are more likely to accept policies and engage with programs over which they have a sense of ownership. And over the long term, regular engagement may build refugees' capacity to take greater ownership over programs and policies in their entirety. Refugee participation comes in many forms, and selecting the appropriate model for an initiative's goals, motivations, and desired outcomes requires careful consideration. To start, as states, UNHCR, and other national and global actors hone their approaches and initiatives for refugee participation, they should develop theories of change and related indicators, and ingrain them within their organizations and communicate them externally. This will give refugee participants a clear idea of how their involvement is expected to affect final decisions and policies, as well as allow for internal learning and external monitoring.

Global, national, and local initiatives to engage refugees in decision-making processes and humanitarian responses generally fall into three categories:

Consultative model: Most current efforts to engage refugees are consultative, whereby a relatively large number of refugees are invited to share their stories and opinions on an ad hoc basis. This light-touch form of engagement allows for the collection of a diversity of viewpoints from people outside the usual policymaking process. However, consultations often involve only surface-level input, which limits both the degree to which the feedback can be informed by and tailored to the process and the extent to which policymakers take refugees' input into consideration.

Advisory model: This approach, which is gaining in popularity, sees refugees serving on advisory boards or as individual advisors, which allows the selected individuals and organizations to continuously engage in a specific policymaking process and provide more sustained, in-depth input. Advisors can leverage their role as outsiders to these processes to bring new perspectives, while also cultivating a deeper understanding of the policymaking process and how to navigate it and developing closer relationships with policymakers than is usually possible via consultations. However, this model tends to favor well-resourced and highly skilled refugees, which limits the diversity of participants and the advice they can offer.

Professional model: Some organizations have appointed refugees to senior leadership positions or hired them as staff, which promises to foster change from within. This is in some ways the ultimate avenue for influence because, as insiders, these refugee professionals can take part in internal discussions about challenging or sensitive issues and serve as liaisons between an organization and their communities in a way that outsiders cannot. However, as is the case for advisory roles, access to professional opportunities is often limited to high-skilled refugees, particularly for senior leadership positions.

The choice of model may depend on the motivations of those seeking input, as well as the resources they have. It should also be noted that these models can be complementary, and that creating multiple entry points for refugee engagement in a process can make it possible to leverage their different benefits in terms of participant diversity and depth of engagement. To strengthen understanding of which models are best suited for different processes and purposes, states, UNHCR, and other global and national actors should pilot a variety of participation models, document these initiatives, and share publicly the information gathered, including reflections on whether and how refugee input was incorporated into final decisions.

Across these models, a range of factors can affect refugees' access to decision-making processes and participants' ability to influence decisions. The degree to which states are willing to engage with refugees often determines whether refugees have access to decision-making fora, at what point in the process, the nature of their involvement, and whether they can speak openly without fearing for their safety. Policymakers often question whether selected refugee participants—who in global fora tend to be younger, English speaking, well-connected, and based in the Global North—legitimately represent the interests and concerns of other refugees, even as the same policymakers may struggle to engage with larger groups that are not structured in ways, they are familiar with and that may present diverging opinions. Access to funding, information, and training are critical for a more diverse group of refugees and refugee-led organizations to engage with policy processes in a way that is sustained and well-informed, and that allows them to identify allies and avenues for influence.

In the absence of democratic structures that represent refugees' public opinion at the global level, states, UNHCR, and other global and national actors should support refugee-led networks in taking steps to guarantee a diversity of participants within the networks. Addressing structural barriers that disproportionately face refugees who are women, minorities, and from the Global South will require long term engagement, resourcing, and training with both refugee-led networks as they work to set up inclusive and effective mechanisms and with emerging advocates from more marginalized groups. Organizations should also include refugees and other people with lived experiences of displacement in their human resources (HR) diversity policies.

In the lead-up to the 2023 Global Refugee Forum, states, UNHCR, and nongovernmental actors alike have an important opportunity to strengthen the links between refugee participation initiatives' goals, their design and operation, and the mechanisms for measuring progress toward the identified goals. Using the theory of change and indicators proposed in this report, stakeholders can foster more thoughtfully designed refugee participation initiatives and ensure that lessons can be drawn and shared. And as refugees become increasingly familiar with policymaking processes and avenues for influence, and as evidence is generated on how best to leverage their contributions, policymakers can move from facilitating refugees' participation toward enabling more equal partnerships.

Paarth Mathur

Integration or Coercion?

Educating refugees through "Citizenship Classes and Tests" is a complex issue that intersects with broader questions of integration, coercion, and autonomous agency. On one hand, these programs can be seen as a tool for integration, designed to equip refugees with the knowledge and skills needed to navigate their new society effectively. On the other hand, there are concerns about whether such requirements act as a form of coercion, potentially undermining the agency of refugees by imposing specific expectations and conditions on their acceptance and integration into the host society.

Proponents argue that citizenship classes and tests serve as an essential mechanism for integration. These programs can:

Provide refugees with crucial information about the legal, social, and cultural norms of their new country.

Enhance language skills, which are vital for social integration, employment, and educational opportunities.

Foster a sense of belonging and citizenship among refugees, encouraging active participation in their new community. However, critics raise concerns about the coercive aspects of mandatory citizenship classes and tests. These concerns include:

The potential for such requirements to marginalize those who struggle with language barriers or learning disabilities. The risk of creating additional stress and pressure on refugees who are already navigating the challenges of displacement and resettlement. Questions about the fairness and relevance of the content covered in citizenship tests, and whether it truly reflects the knowledge needed to participate in society.

Autonomous Agency

Another critical aspect of this debate revolves around the concept of autonomous agency—the capacity of refugees to make their own choices and decisions regarding their integration process. Supporters of citizenship classes and tests may argue that these programs empower refugees by providing them with the tools and knowledge needed to succeed in their new country. In contrast, critics might contend that imposing these requirements restricts refugees' autonomy by delineating a predetermined path to integration.

Balancing Integration and Autonomy

Finding a balance between promoting integration and respecting the autonomy of refugees is crucial. Some potential approaches to achieve this balance could include offering voluntary participation in citizenship classes, with incentives rather than mandates.

Tailoring programs to meet the diverse needs and backgrounds of refugees, acknowledging that a one-size-fits-all approach may not be effective.

Engaging refugees in the development and evaluation of citizenship programs to ensure they are relevant, respectful, and empowering.

In conclusion, the debate over educating refugees through citizenship classes and tests highlights the tension between the goals of integration and the respect for individual autonomy. Striking the right balance requires thoughtful consideration of the needs, rights, and perspectives of refugees, ensuring that such programs support rather than undermine their journey towards successful integration.

Opportunities

Multilingual communities play a crucial role in preserving heritage languages, offering a unique blend of cultural identity and linguistic diversity. These communities serve as vital spaces where individuals can maintain and celebrate their ancestral languages alongside the dominant language of their residing country. Heritage languages are not just a means of communication but also a connection to cultural heritage, traditions, and history. By fostering multilingual environments, societies can enrich cultural understanding, promote diversity, and support the intergenerational transmission of linguistic knowledge.

Newcomer populations are often more easily accepted when they share core characteristics (ethnic, religious, or cultural similarities) and/or a common language with the host population. Visibly different groups tend to elicit greater fears that newcomers are eroding the social fabric or making irrevocable changes to lifestyles, traditions, and even the face of communities (as can happen when newcomers of different religions build new places of worship), particularly in places new to diversity and immigration. At times, this effect can be racialized. For instance, the 'great replacement theory' rhetoric by right-wing nationalist politicians, which weaponizes fears of non-White newcomers taking over or displacing native-born people, has become prominent in places such as Italy and the United States.

Perceived proximity played a key role in the strong support for Ukrainians in Europe, as some leaders and media commentators highlighted their Europeanness and cultural similarities. Particularly in some countries in Eastern and Central Europe, this contrasted with the negative perceptions of refugees coming from other parts of the world, who were instead perceived as a threat. Already in 2015–16, a survey conducted in Poland found that 60 per cent of Poles would accept refugees from Ukraine, but only one-quarter would welcome refugees coming from Africa and the Middle East. While this difference was not as stark in Western Europe, a survey conducted in the Netherlands, Belgium, France, and Sweden in 2017 also found that public opinion towards refugees from a different ethnicity or from non-European countries was less favorable than that towards refugees with ethnic and cultural ties. Meanwhile, in Turkey, religious proximity facilitated solidarity towards Syrians fleeing war, with President Erdoğan asking Turkish citizens to help their 'Muslim brothers and sisters'. And in Colombia, former president Iván Duque announced the historic legalization of Venezuelans in the country in 2021, referring to Venezuelans as 'brothers.

Geographic proximity can also significantly drive solidarity, which can overlap with racial or ethnic ties. Shared borders facilitate important cultural and economic links, common geostrategic interests, and cross-border mobility, and evidence shows that direct contact between host and refugee populations can play an important role in generating positive attitudes. In Europe, several countries, particularly those neighboring Ukraine, had a large Ukrainian diaspora before the war. This nurtured a sense of familiarity and made the mobilization of the diaspora key in the displacement response, with almost one-third of displaced Ukrainians having reported staying with friends and family by June 2022. Geographic proximity can also lead to a shared history that can be tapped to fuel solidarity. In Colombia, the collective memory of Colombians emigrating to Venezuela was mobilized to encourage support, and in Turkey, the government referred to a common Ottoman past to highlight proximity to those coming from Syria. Neighboring countries also often have shared political interests, including common political adversaries. In Central and Eastern Europe, the memory of being part of the Soviet Union and the perception of Russia as a common enemy was a key element in the strong solidarity towards Ukrainians. Ukrainians were thus perceived as allies, standing with Poles against Russians, who had in the past posed a threat to Polish identity. The impact of having a perceived shared enemy is also illustrated in polls: a survey conducted in

Voices: Linguistic and Cultural Dynamics of Refugee Population in America

Czechia, for instance, found that 84 per cent of those blaming Russia for the war were in favor of welcoming Ukrainian refugees, compared to 8 per cent who believed the war was caused by NATO and 2 per cent who pointed the finger at the United States.

Therefore, shared historic and cultural ties with newcomers can mean they are more likely to be perceived as part of 'us' and not a threatening 'other'. In some instances, policymakers have leveraged this in a selective manner; for example, Turkey's president emphasized shared religion to rally support for Syrians, while omitting the ethnic differences between Turks and Syrians. At the same time, focusing on similar characteristics or fraternal ties to mobilize support is a double-edged sword. While it can drive solidarity when refugees are culturally, ethnically, or religiously similar to host populations, it can also reinforce the perception that other migrant and refugee groups are less deserving of solidarity. Moreover, proximity alone is not sufficient to maintain public support over time. Despite the religious and cultural similarities between Venezuelans and Colombians and between Turks and Syrians, these countries have still seen rapid deterioration of public attitudes and a growing perception of these refugee populations as threats to the host countries' identity and culture. Therefore, other pieces of the puzzle, such as effective integration policies that foster social cohesion, need to be in place as well for solidarity to remain strong over time.

Pragmatism Displaced populations typically seek safety close by, especially if they plan to return home eventually, if they already have the legal right to cross a particular border, or if there is an existing diaspora community that can initially support them. This explains why 69 per cent of the world's refugees are hosted in neighboring countries.

Thus, a sense of pragmatism can drive some welcoming responses: displaced populations have few other options, and it can be impractical (or simply unfeasible) to turn away people who have long enjoyed cross-border mobility. For instance, before the conflict in Ukraine, Ukrainians had the right to stay in the European Union for 90 days without a visa, which meant that EU countries could not legally prevent the massive influx of Ukrainians crossing their borders. The activation of the TPD also had another pragmatic element, which was to avoid the collapse of already-overstretched asylum systems as might have occurred if countries had been forced to individually process applications for millions of people. And for Colombia, which shares long, porous borders of more than 2,000 kilometers with Venezuela, it was simply not realistic to close the border and fully stop migrant arrivals, without sweeping political and economic ramifications. The regularization of Venezuelans in the country in 2021 also aimed to reduce the large proportion of migrants living in the shadows. These cases illustrate that developing inclusive responses, for instance by establishing prima facie refugee determination or other automatic forms of group protection, can become a political calculation to manage arrivals in an orderly manner and mitigate negative impacts such as scenes of chaos at the border, extreme pressure on reception and asylum systems, or growing numbers of irregular migrants living in the country. Developing pragmatic responses can, in turn, positively impact public support, since attitudes often do not depend on the number of arrivals but on how arrivals are managed.

Values Some countries have linked support for refugees to national values or national pride. For instance, politicians in Colombia have emphasized the social value of hosting refugees and developing a generous humanitarian policy, and the Turkish rhetoric of hospitality and the Islamic values of compassion have been used to garner support for Syrians. Turkish politicians have also invoked their generous welcome of refugees as a source of pride on the international stage. And in Poland, some observers have argued that supporting Ukrainians became an element of social desirability and that it had become 'in fashion' for Poles to talk about how they were helping Ukrainians and hosting refugees at home. In this way, support became something that contributed to social status and self-esteem.

Voices: Linguistic and Cultural Dynamics of Refugee Population in America

Narratives about 'deserving' refugees can also impact initial solidarity. In many countries, refugees are perceived in the public imagination as vulnerable, and helping them taps into humanitarian values of compassion. But people who do not fit the image of being vulnerable are more likely to be perceived as bogus, or fake, refugees. In Europe, for example, the overrepresentation of women and children in the Ukrainian refugee population fit the image of deserving refugees in some countries, driving public support. At the same time, these types of narratives can also be used to fuel anti-refugee sentiment, as they can create opposition towards refugees who fall outside of this constructed image of how refugees should look or behave. For instance, in Poland, fringe discourse against Ukrainians on social media platforms has emphasized that some Ukrainians do not need help, for instance by highlighting their expensive shopping habits. And in Turkey, the arrival of mostly young men was a factor in the growing perception of Syrian refugees as a security concern. In addition to social values, individual values can influence attitudes towards refugees. Party politics, for instance, have been found to affect attitudes towards Ukrainians in some European countries. In Colombia, a study has shown that political fears can drive negative attitudes, as those who perceived Venezuelan migrants to be left-wing were less likely to support welcoming policies. This finding is in line with several studies that have found a link between individual values such as universalism and conservatism and attitudes towards migration. Tapping into social values, when these are inclusive, can be an effective way to nurture a more welcoming attitude towards migrants and refugees and to avoid narrowing solidarity to those who are culturally or religiously close to native-born individuals. Germany, for instance, drew on its Willkommenskultur, or welcome culture, during the 2015–16 large-scale arrivals of Syrians-a culturally, religiously, and ethnically different population-to encourage support for refugees. At the same time, even if leveraging a sense of national pride or social duty can nurture initial solidarity, support is likely to gradually deteriorate unless policymakers also address public anxieties related to welcoming and integrating new arrivals, which often increase after the emergency phase.

There is often an unspoken limit to the level of sacrifice that the public is willing to make, either in terms of what is being offered or for how long. Solidarity towards refugees does not translate to the provision of blanket support, and some measures, such as access to health care, can rally more support than other benefits that are not shared by locals or that might fuel specific fears of direct competition, such as access to the labor market. Moreover, willingness to maintain the same level of support often wanes over time. If the public does not see refugees as contributing to society, they can be gradually perceived as a burden on public resources, particularly if the host population is experiencing economic insecurity.

98

Paarth Mathur

What factors can erode public support and cause compassion fatigue?

Even in situations where solidarity is initially high, practical concerns will eventually begin to bump up against the limits of what people are willing to sacrifice. The rush of solidarity that can come from a crisis or emergency setting the feeling of 'we're all in it together' and 'everyone has to do their part' is difficult to sustain indefinitely, especially if the public perceives that the burden is not being shared evenly and that local and national governments, or the international community, are not doing their fair share. In Colombia and Turkey, the initial solidarity towards Venezuelans and Syrians has deteriorated significantly in recent years, as the issue of continuing support has become increasingly contentious. In Europe, overall support for Ukrainians remains high 18 months after the start of the war, but some cracks have begun to show as host communities begin to worry about long-term impacts. Understanding the conditions that lead attitudes to deteriorate over time can help policymakers sustain solidarity and prevent public backlash.

Anti-immigrant rhetoric often falsely associates refugees with crime and economic burdens, overlooking their long-term economic contributions. Public campaigns can refute these myths, but appealing to humanitarian values and encouraging interactions between locals and refugees are more impactful.

Perceptions of unfairness Large displaced populations are often seen as exacerbating existing problems in host societies, such as housing or job scarcity. Publics generally support granting refugees' access to basic public benefits, but there is often a limit to this support, especially if publics feel that refugees are getting more than marginalized or impoverished native-born people. In Slovakia, for instance, almost 60 per cent of people surveyed in 2022 believed that the government treated Ukrainians better than Slovakians, which can explain why, compared to respondents in other surveyed countries, those in Slovakia were keener to reduce support for Ukrainians, and in contrast to all other countries, the majority did not support welcoming Ukrainians. Perceptions of unfairness can be exacerbated when migrants and refugees receive targeted benefits not shared by the wider population or when the public perceives that newcomers receive more than they contribute. In a context of widespread housing shortages and rising housing costs that have sparked protests across Europe, a survey conducted in four European countries found that the provision of subsidized housing to Ukrainians was generally unpopular.106 In Colombia, programs that target Venezuelans exclusively are considered politically infeasible, given not only the widespread economic hardship in the country but also existing requirements to earmark services for internally displaced Colombians. Thus, favoring policy interventions that can benefit the whole population, for instance investing in affordable housing for all, instead of measures that target only refugees holds potential to avoid flashpoints for tensions between refugees and host populations.

Policymakers have faced pressure to enact policies that reflect a transition to more-equitable burden sharing between hosts and newcomers. Poland, for example, announced in November 2022 that Ukrainians who stayed in reception centers for more than 120 days would be charged 50 per cent of the costs, up to 40 zlotys (approx. 9 euros) per day. And as a growing number of Ukrainian refugees have also returned to Ukraine (whether permanently or temporarily), several European governments have announced that they are taking measures to ensure that people do not take advantage of benefits while not in EU territory, measures arguably driven not just by fiscal prudence but also by the desire to reduce perceptions that some Ukrainians are 'gaming the system'. These strategies can therefore act as a signal to the public and mitigate perceptions of unfairness. Yet, cutting support to refugees, especially if they are in a vulnerable position, can delay integration and have important negative economic and social consequences down the line. For that reason, governments need to strike the right balance between supporting new arrivals, so they successfully integrate in host societies and ensuring they are not perceived as taking advantage of the system.

The feeling of burden can be seen clearly in border communities that feel disproportionately affected by largescale arrivals. A survey conducted in Eastern and Central Europe found that people living in cross-border areas were more likely to have negative views towards Ukrainians and, due to their arrival, perceive negative changes to their own lives. In Poland, for instance, 29 per cent of respondents residing in border areas said their lives had been negatively affected by those fleeing Ukraine, compared to 13 per cent of all respondents. In Colombia, negative attitudes towards Venezuelans also concentrate in areas with a high number of arrivals, including regions close to the border. To mitigate negative attitudes, policymakers should focus on measures that promote a more even distribution of the impact, for example through the relocation of new arrivals to other parts of the territory or by providing additional support to disproportionally affected communities.

Perception of being displaced or left behind Perceptions of unfairness may also increase for segments of the population who are (or perceive themselves to be) in direct competition with newcomers, for instance workers in the industries in which migrant workers are overrepresented or individuals facing housing insecurity. This perception emerges in many surveys showing that native-born people with lower socioeconomic status are generally more likely to perceive the arrival of refugees as an economic threat. In Czechia, for example, respondents identifying themselves as having average income and poorer households were more likely to say they experienced negative changes due to the influx of refugees. Similarly, in Slovakia, respondents from poorer households were more likely to believe that support for Ukrainians should be reduced.112 And in Colombia, negative attitudes towards Venezuelans have been particularly prominent in border areas with pre-existing public service capacity shortages and that have received a high number of Venezuelans.

Voices: Linguistic and Cultural Dynamics of Refugee Population in America

This fear of newcomers often hinges on a perception of resources as a zero-sum game, in which people believe that granting benefits to newcomers will result in reduction of benefits for native-born people. For instance, in Colombia, access to the labor market has been more contentious than access to other services such as education, amid fears of Venezuelans taking jobs from natives. In Austria, more than one third of respondents in several surveys conducted in 2022 expressed fears that the arrival of Ukrainians would make it more difficult for Austrians to find jobs. This finding is also why solidarity campaigns that frame refugees as victims in need of support can sometimes backfire, as some public anxiety directly relates to the perception that newcomers will be a burden on the receiving society and that they will take away resources from native-born individuals. Thus, instead of focusing on changing negative attitudes by promoting positive narratives, policymakers should focus first on addressing concrete, day-to-day concerns, for instance increasing investments in overstretched public services or working towards decreasing the unemployment rate of both refugees and locals.

Uncertainty about the future The Colombian and Turkish case studies are illustrative not just because of the sheer volume of arrivals over time but also because of the inherent uncertainty surrounding these movements. Both Venezuelans and Syrians came in successive waves over a period of multiple years with no discernible end to the displacement. And in both cases, the public initially believed newcomers would eventually return to their countries of origin. It is arguably harder for people to give indefinite or open-ended support, compared to a situation in which the size of the challenge (and resources needed to address it) is known from the beginning. In Turkey, welcoming attitudes were linked to the fact that Syrians were seen as temporary guests, but as the situation became protracted and the guests slowly became more-permanent residents, attitudes took a negative turn. While solidarity for Ukrainians in Europe has remained overwhelmingly positive, there are also signs that this support will be difficult to sustain permanently. For example, in Poland, a survey in

August 2022 found that while 87 per cent of Poles supported helping refugees in the first few months of the war, less than one-third (31 per cent) agreed that Poland should support Ukrainians for the entire duration of the conflict. Similarly, a 2023 survey in Czechia found that only 9 per cent of citizens were in favor of Ukrainians staying permanently in the country, while almost two-thirds (64 per cent) favored temporary admission. When the initial period of emergency displacement begins to stretch into something more permanent, it is also more difficult for donors and citizens to maintain the same level of material support. Many Europeans opened their homes to Ukrainians as millions fled the conflict, but a year later, the willingness of hosts to maintain this support had decreased. In Poland, 63 per cent of Poles indicated in 2022 that they were personally supporting Ukrainians, which dropped to 41 per cent in January 2023, and this figure is likely to continue decreasing. In some emergency situations that become protracted, the diminishing willingness (or ability) of citizens to personally support refugees over time can overlap with donors decreasing their funding or technical support to host countries. This can create a shortfall for governments, which can struggle to maintain the same level of support for refugees, and stretched resources can, in turn, potentially fuel negative attitudes if the host population starts feeling that their guests are, instead, competitors.

Therefore, while leveraging diaspora or public support in the initial stages of a mass displacement crisis can quickly scale up capacity to meet the needs of new arrivals, governments should have a plan to take over these responsibilities after the initial phase of the emergency has passed, to avoid solidarity burnout. Uncertainty about the future, however, also poses an important challenge for governments, which often have the competing policy objectives of promoting the longer-term integration of migrants and refugees while preparing for the eventual return of part of the refugee population to their countries of origin. Adopting a dual-intent approach that can prepare refugees both for integration and for eventual return, for instance by investing in upskilling in sectors relevant to both the host and the origin countries, can be a way to navigate this context of uncertainty and ease public worries that the government is focusing only on the longer-term stay of newcomers.

Perception of lack of control over migration

Publics all over the world tend to express a desire for orderly and managed migration, and support often hinges on whether they perceive migration as managed effectively regardless of the number of arrivals. When arrivals appear chaotic or refugees are not perceived to be integrating into a society, perceptions of refugees as a threat can increase. In the Greek islands, for instance, the high number of refugee arrivals in 2015–16 and perceptions that the arrivals' impact fell disproportionally on the island communities led to the local population's growing resistance. In Colombia, growing negative attitudes have correlated with negative perceptions of the government's management of Venezuelan migration. And in Austria, support for Ukrainians fell over the course of the past year as concerns about their integration gradually increased.

Consequently, policy responses that promote orderly arrivals can create a sense of control and mitigate public anxieties. The perception of threat, for instance, has been lower in Europe with the arrival of millions of Ukrainians than in 2015–16, when the arrival of 1 million refugees threw Europe into a state of disarray. There are many factors behind these different perceptions, but the European Union's swift response to manage arrivals and grant them access to immediate protection arguably provided a sense of control that was missing in 2015–16. Yet, this type of group-determination responses also hinges on its political viability, and it will be difficult to justify politically if widespread public support towards those who are displaced does not already exist.

Paarth Mathur

Sense of existential threat

Cultural and demographic concerns tend to become especially salient for host communities during certain transition periods, for instance when the demographic balance is set to shift or when newcomers gain benefits (such as voting) with which they are seen as able to exercise outsized influence on a society's cultural, religious, or linguistic trajectory. These transitions can also occur when refugees shift from being seen as temporary guests to permanent members of society. A high fertility rate among refugees can also raise concerns about demographic change; for instance, while the average fertility rate in Turkey is 1.9 children per woman, it is 5.3 for Syrians. Once the realization sets in that refugees' demographic and political clout is growing (and may alter the demographic, political, or religious balance) and that they are not likely to return to their countries of origin, new threat frames may emerge. In Turkey, despite the government's emphasis on the religious similarities and shared history between Turks and Syrians, a 2020 study found that 82 per cent of Turks felt that they had no cultural commonalities with Syrians. The welcome may have been balanced delicately on the political promise of Syrians as "guests". Important nuances also underlie the umbrella of 'Muslim brotherhood'. For Turkey's more secular population, Syrian migration may be linked to a threat of Islamification, while for Turkey's religious minorities, Sunni Arab Syrians can be perceived as a demographic threat that can tip the scale in favor of the ruling party in some regions and marginalize some communities.

Conclusion

The concept of "Vasudhaiva Kutumbakam," a Sanskrit phrase
meaning "the world is one family," epitomizes the
interconnectedness and shared responsibilities of humanity. This
philosophy is particularly pertinent in the context of refugees, who
embody the challenges and potential of global unity.

Refugees are people displaced from their home region for a particular
reason, whether that ube war, religious persecution, violence with
gangs in their home country, etc. The modern refugee was
first established in 1951 with the making of the United Nations
Convention Relating to the status of refugees and grew with the 1967
protocol expanding to protect all refugees, while the 1951
conventions only protected European immigrants. Finally, in 1980
the U.S passed its immigration act, passed by Jimmy Carter, detailing
the the procedure for refugee admission into the U.S, leading to the
development of the refugee state we see today. However, contrary
to popular belief, the U.S does not house the most refugees. That
honor belongs to Iran, followed by Turkey, then Germany, etc. The
U.S does not even crack the top ten. And with 100 million refugees
and other internationally displaced people, the U. S's capacity and
resources to be able to house these refugees further accentuates the
failure of America to manage these refugees. And with political
legislature limiting the influx of immigrants due to new architectural
monuments, the immigration into the U.S is seeming more limited
than ever. New legislature must be passed in order to place fear away
from a misguided belief that refugees will take jobs away from
native-born citizens, when that has not been the case at all. In fact,
refugees create jobs as they expand the labor system and the
economy.

Refugees were responsible for a total of 123.8 billion
dollars fiscally for the U.S government, creating more incentive for
the U.S to encourage refugee influx. Refugees in America also face
many problems. Only a fraction of immigrants in the US are LEP, or
limited English proficient, with the main leaders being immigrants

from Mexico, China, Vietnam, Cuba, etc. For refugees in countries that do not learn English as closely or are as associated with the U.S, it becomes very difficult in order to be able to communicate effectively in the country. Additionally, the transfer of refugees from their home country can be difficult. It can be difficult to grow accustomed to a completely new environment and culture, especially one as big and busy as the US.

There are 4 phases to the arrival of a refugee:
The honeymoon phase, or the initial feeling of excitement. The culture shock phase, or stress and homesickness that result from trying to integrate into another culture. The adjustment phase, or when they begin to form routines and adjust. The mastery phase, or comfortability in the new environment, though some difficulty will still happen.

Even with completing these phases, the inability to communicate can make it harder for refugees to secure high-paying jobs, and therefore afford better and more secure housing. They also struggle to access services in fear of being deported. So, in support and to propagate refugee settlement, there are 3 models that are commonly used to support integration. The first model was the consultative model, a very popular model that allow refugees to share their stories and talk freely about their opinions, allowing for more varied opinions on a variety of issues. The other 2 focus more on facilitating the needs of refugee populations. The facilitation of refugees into a home country and their involvement in it is invaluable in creating a better and more varied state.

The plight of refugees gained global prominence after World War II, leading to the 1951 United Nations Convention Relating to the Status of Refugees. This convention, expanded by the 1967 Protocol, established a framework for protecting refugees, defining them as individuals fleeing persecution based on race, religion, nationality, political opinion, or membership in a particular social group. The Refugee Act of 1980 further aligned U.S. law with these international standards, creating a structured approach to refugee resettlement and support. The establishment of these international agreements marked a turning point for refugees, offering a framework for their protection and rights. For many refugees, including the Al-Mansours, a family of three who fled their war-torn homeland in the Middle East in 1951, these conventions provided a lifeline. The Al-Mansours' journey, from a refugee camp in Germany to resettlement in the United States, underscores the resilience and adaptability required to rebuild lives in new lands.

Language is a fundamental aspect of identity and plays a crucial role in the integration process for refugees. The ability to communicate in the host country's language is essential for accessing education, employment, and social services. However, the journey to linguistic proficiency is fraught with challenges. Refugees often face difficulties learning English due to limited access to educational resources, pre-existing trauma, and the need to prioritize immediate survival needs over language acquisition. Despite these challenges, linguistic diversity within refugee communities enriches the cultural fabric of the host society. Multilingualism allows for the preservation of cultural heritage and facilitates communication within diverse communities. Programs aimed at teaching English as a Second Language (ESL) are vital, yet they must be complemented by support systems that address the broader socio-economic barriers refugees face.

Cultural adaptation involves a delicate balance between preserving one's heritage and embracing new cultural norms. Refugees often navigate a complex landscape of maintaining their native traditions while integrating into American society. This process can be particularly challenging for youth, who must reconcile the cultural expectations of their families with those of their peers. Events such as culturally sensitive baby showers, as described by Mathur, demonstrate the potential for community initiatives to bridge cultural gaps. These events provide a platform for sharing and celebrating diverse traditions, fostering a sense of belonging and mutual respect. During my humanitarian mission in Peru, I had the opportunity to work in a medical facility and witness firsthand the resilience and adaptability of refugees. This experience underscored the importance of providing support and creating inclusive environments for displaced populations. I also participated in organizing a baby shower for refugee women in our community, which highlighted the significance of cultural sensitivity and the power of shared experiences in fostering community bonds.

Refugees encounter numerous barriers to integration, including language barriers, educational challenges, employment obstacles, housing issues, and access to services. Limited English proficiency can impede access to essential services and employment opportunities. Refugee children often struggle in school due to language difficulties and differing educational backgrounds. Refugees may face discrimination and exploitation in the job market, with professional qualifications from their home countries often not recognized. Finding affordable and safe housing is a significant challenge, exacerbated by economic constraints and potential exploitation by landlords. Navigating healthcare, legal, and social services can be daunting, especially for those unfamiliar with the systems and language. My personal experiences working with refugees have shown me the immense barriers they face. For instance, I witnessed a refugee family in Houston struggling to navigate the healthcare system due to language barriers, which resulted in delayed medical treatment for a child with a serious condition. Such experiences highlight the urgent need for improved support systems to aid refugees in overcoming these barriers.

Effective integration requires a multifaceted approach, including enhanced language programs, cultural orientation sessions, community support networks, and policy advocacy. Comprehensive ESL programs tailored to different age groups and literacy levels are essential. Pre-arrival and ongoing cultural orientation can reduce culture shock and facilitate smoother transitions. Initiatives that connect refugees with local communities foster mutual understanding and support. Efforts to ensure policies are inclusive and supportive of refugee needs, including recognition of foreign qualifications and protection against discrimination, are crucial. My involvement with refugee support programs in Houston has shown me the importance of these multifaceted approaches. For example, the cultural orientation sessions we conducted for new arrivals significantly eased their transition into American society. These sessions covered everything from understanding public transportation to navigating the education system, providing refugees with the tools they needed to start their new lives with confidence.

The integration of refugees enriches host societies with a tapestry of linguistic and cultural diversity, sparking innovation, economic growth, and a deeper understanding among communities. By bringing unique traditions, skills, and perspectives, refugees contribute to the social fabric in myriad ways, from enhancing the arts and cuisine to fueling business innovation and enriching educational environments. Government policies aimed at supporting refugees' integration are crucial as they not only help individuals rebuild their lives but also unlock the potential benefits of diversity for the broader society. Such policies should focus on language education, employment opportunities, and access to health and social services, fostering an environment where both refugees and host communities can thrive together in mutual respect and cooperation.

The linguistic landscape of refugee populations vividly encapsulates the hurdles and complex situations these groups encounter as they adjust to new sociocultural settings. Marked by a rich diversity, continual evolution, and the capacity for adaptation, this linguistic scenario mirrors larger stories of movement, self-identity, and endurance. It highlights the significant role language plays in refugee experiences, from overcoming communication obstacles to seizing chances for cultural enrichment and forging community ties. Acknowledging and addressing the language requirements and assets of refugees is crucial for developing welcoming societies that honor and value diversity.

Migration also plays a crucial role in the preservation and evolution of languages. Diaspora communities often become custodians of their native languages, passing them down through generations as a connection to their ancestral roots. At the same time, these languages evolve, blending with others and incorporating new influences to create dynamic, living dialects that reflect the hybrid identities of their speakers. For instance, the emergence of Spanglish in the United States or Hinglish in the United Kingdom highlights how languages morph and adapt in multicultural contexts. In a world characterized by diverse cultures and languages, sign languages stand as unique and vibrant forms of communication for millions of individuals worldwide. With an estimated 300 different sign languages across the globe, these visual-spatial languages are the lifeblood of deaf communities, providing a means to express thoughts, emotions, and ideas.

Sign languages are complete, natural languages with their own grammatical rules, syntax, and vocabulary. Unlike spoken languages, which utilize sound, sign languages employ a rich array of handshapes, facial expressions, body movements, and spatial cues to convey meaning. These languages can be used for everyday conversations, storytelling, academic pursuits, artistic expression, and cultural preservation. The global distribution of sign languages reflects the diversity of the deaf communities they serve. For instance, American Sign Language (ASL) is predominantly used in the United States and parts of Canada, British Sign Language (BSL) in the United Kingdom, and Australian Sign Language (Auslan) in Australia. Each sign language is regionally and culturally specific, with distinct characteristics that highlight the unique experiences of their users. Sign languages play a crucial role in fostering a sense of belonging, enabling cultural preservation, and providing a platform for artistic expression within deaf communities. They facilitate the transmission of folklore, storytelling, and historical narratives, allowing deaf individuals to connect with their heritage and celebrate their unique identity.

Voices: Linguistic and Cultural Dynamics of Refugee Population in America

Recognizing the importance of sign languages in ensuring equal participation and access for deaf individuals, efforts are being made to promote their recognition and accessibility. Technology plays a vital role in facilitating communication between sign language users and non-signers, such as through video relay services and sign language translation apps. Education systems are gradually incorporating sign language as a subject, creating a more inclusive learning environment. The vast array of sign languages worldwide is a testament to the linguistic and cultural diversity of deaf communities. Each sign language represents a unique expression of identity and provides a powerful means of communication and connection within its respective community. As we continue to strive for a more inclusive and accessible world, recognizing and supporting sign languages will be essential in fostering equality, diversity, and cultural understanding.

In an increasingly interconnected world, understanding and celebrating cultural diversity is more important than ever. I recently had the privilege of organizing a baby shower for a group of refugee women in our community. This event was not just a celebration of impending motherhood but also an eye-opening journey into the rich tapestry of cultural diversity. Through this experience, I gained invaluable insights into the challenges, joys, and resilience of people from diverse backgrounds. The idea was born out of a desire to support and empower refugee women who often face numerous challenges as they navigate their new lives in unfamiliar surroundings. Recognizing that pregnancy and motherhood are universal experiences that can transcend cultural and linguistic barriers, we saw an opportunity to bring together women from different backgrounds in a celebration that could foster community and support.

Planning the baby shower required careful consideration and cultural sensitivity. We collaborated with community leaders, conducted online research, and engaged the women themselves to ensure that the event was respectful of their cultural norms and preferences. This collaboration was enlightening, as it exposed me to various cultural practices and traditions related to pregnancy and childbirth. We decided on a neutral theme that celebrated new life, using decorations and symbols that were inclusive and representative of the various cultures of the participants.

The movement of refugees, migrants, and immigrants is a testament to the resilience and diversity of the human spirit. Through their languages, they carry the stories of their journeys, struggles, and hopes, weaving them into the fabric of their new communities. As the world continues to navigate the complexities of migration, it's clear that languages will remain at the forefront of discussions on identity, culture, and belonging. By embracing linguistic diversity, we can build more inclusive societies that recognize the value of every voice and the richness it brings to our collective human experience.

Being on the margins can fuel creative innovation. Individuals exposed to multiple cultures from a young age often conceive a wider array of human emotions and life experiences, such as love, loss, and family dynamics. This experience of marginality, especially when paired with remarkable talent and a keen sense for art, fosters a heightened receptivity to new ideas and innovations.

VASUDHAIVA KUTUMBAKAM
"THE WORLD IS A FAMILY"

Appendix

REFUGEE RESETTLEMENT FACTS

October 2023

Refugee: A person forced to flee their home country to escape war, violence or persecution.

Resettlement: Refugees who are resettled go to another country that has agreed to admit them and ultimately grant them permanent residence.

Why is refugee resettlement important? Resettlement is a life-saving solution for the most vulnerable refugees in the world, and is also an important way to share responsibility and support the countries that host the majority of the world's refugees.

5 THINGS TO KNOW ABOUT REFUGEE RESETTLEMENT

1. Refugees do not apply for resettlement themselves. UNHCR identifies vulnerable cases to be considered for resettlement.

2. Only the most vulnerable refugees are considered. All refugees who are referred must fit at least one category, some of which include:

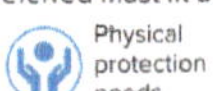 Physical protection needs

 Survivors of violence or torture

 Women & girls at risk

3. Countries decide which refugees to admit for resettlement.

4. Persons who have committed serious crimes or who might pose a security threat are not eligible for refugee status or resettlement.

5. Refugee resettlement saves lives.

RESETTLEMENT TO THE U.S. IN FISCAL YEAR 2023

The United States has a long history of welcoming refugees and has historically been one of the largest refugee resettlement countries in the world. FY2023 data covers October 2022 - September 2023.

TOP STATES FOR RESETTLEMENT

47 states received refugees for resettlement

REFUGEES RESETTLED TO THE U.S. BY REGION OF ORIGIN*

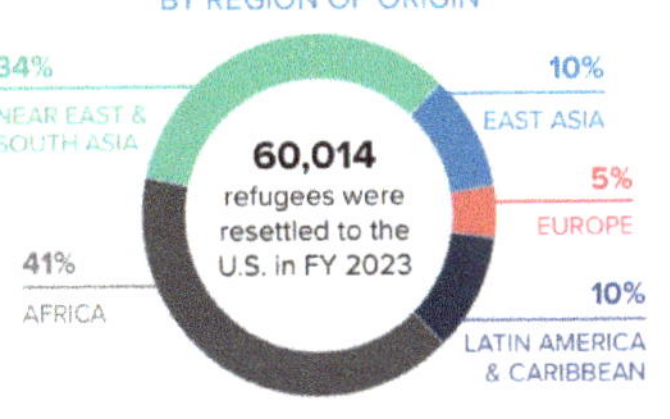

Includes refugees resettled with and without UNHCR assistance

2022 GLOBAL FIGURES AT A GLANCE

There are **35.3 million** refugees worldwide

Only **1 in 309** are resettled

24 countries around the world accepted refugee resettlement submissions from 84 different countries of origin.

1.5 million refugees are in need of resettlement but **only 7% were resettled.**

U.S. RESETTLEMENT PROCESS

In addition to UNHCR's screening, the U.S. conducts its own vetting process to decide whether to accept a refugee for resettlement. The entire process can take up to 2 years.

 UNHCR and NGO partners refer a refugee to be considered for resettlement and provides detailed background information.

 The U.S. government screens the refugee and decides whether to admit them for resettlement. This process includes:

8 U.S. government agencies
5 Separate security databases
6 Background checks
2 In-person interviews

If the refugee is approved, the State Department assigns the case to one of 10 U.S. NGOs or a private sponsor.

 Travel arrangements are coordinated by the International Organization for Migration and partners.

 The NGO or private sponsor welcomes the refugee and helps them integrate and become economically self-sufficient in their new U.S. community.

U.S. REFUGEE ADMISSIONS CEILING

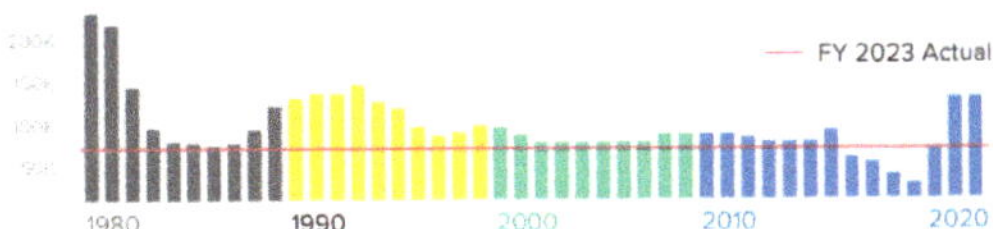

TOP COUNTRIES OF ORIGIN FOR REFUGEES RESETTLED TO THE U.S.

1. Democratic Republic of Congo
2. Syria
3. Afghanistan
4. Myanmar

Sources: U.S. Department of State; Department of Health and Human Services; UNHCR | unhcr.org/us/ | @UNHCRUSA

Ukraine Refugee Crisis

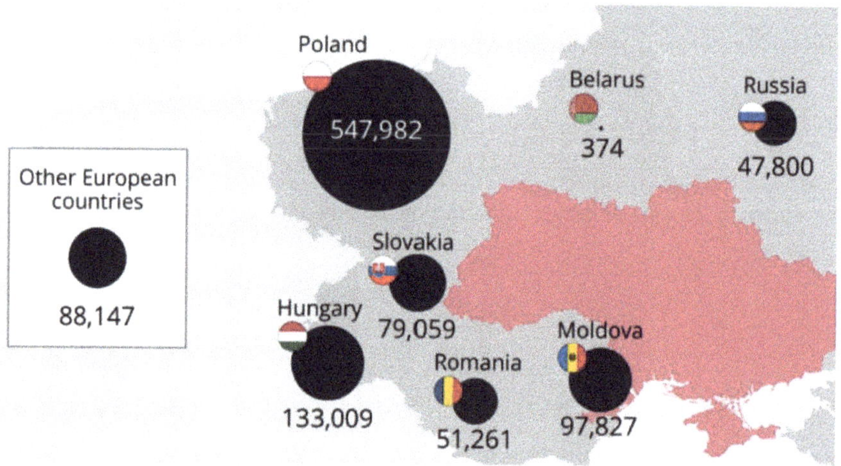

As of 3 March, more than half of the 3 million Ukrainian refugees have arrived in Poland.

Image: Statista

The Russian Federation's full-scale invasion of Ukraine in February 2022 uprooted millions of people who fled into neighboring countries and beyond as refugees, in addition to millions more who were displaced within the country. While the peak of the displacement occurred during the first four months of the full-scale invasion, population movements from and to Ukraine have continued ever since and become more complex. On the one hand, the ongoing full-scale war and hostilities across the country continue to force people to flee in search of safety. On the other, many refugees engage in pendular movements and short-term visits between Ukraine and host countries, and others have voluntarily returned to Ukraine on a more permanent basis. This analysis brings together available evidence from different sources to build a comprehensive picture of the situation for informed decision-making, highlighting remaining data gaps.

After the massive flight of refugees in the first months of the full-scale war, border crossings from and to the western borders of Ukraine have tended to stabilize over time, with more than 1 million monthly movements from and to Ukraine (each) during 2023, according to data shared by national authorities in host countries neighboring Ukraine.

While in general the number of crossings from Ukraine has exceeded the number of crossings back into the country for most weeks and months, this has fluctuated in certain periods, particularly during winter or summer holidays.

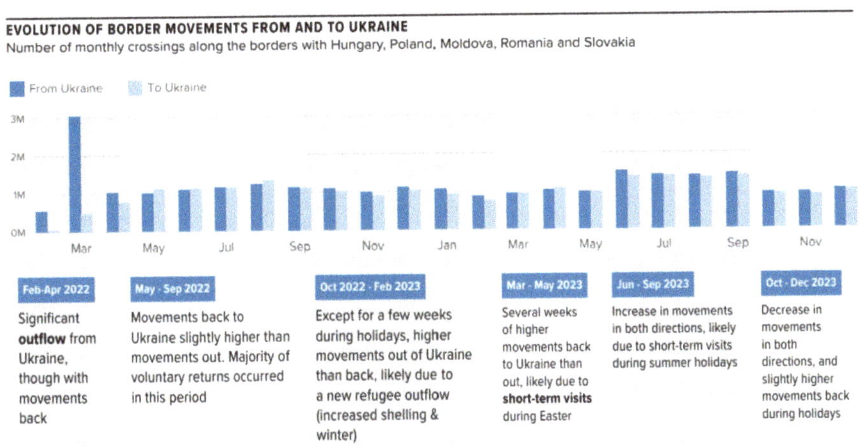

Source: Border authorities in Hungary, Poland, Moldova, Romania and Slovakia. Data does not include crossings of nationals of the bordering countries.

How many refugees are engaging in pendular movements and short-term visits?

The Ukraine refugee crisis is characterized by high levels of family separation. As expected in this context, the most frequent reasons reported by refugees for travelling back to Ukraine are to visit relatives or friends, followed by access to healthcare and to obtain documentation. Short-term visits are more frequent among refugees hosted in neighboring countries. Moreover, visits have been more frequent among refugees originating from the West, the Centre or the North of Ukraine, particularly among those with an undamaged home in Ukraine. Surveys have further highlighted that 40% of refugees were unable to visit Ukraine even if they wanted to, due to security concerns or lack of funds, followed by caregiving responsibilities, a lack of documentation and the fear of losing their legal status in host countries.

Data from UNHCR's intentions survey indicates an increasing trend in short-term visits over time, with up to 39% of refugees (around 1.8 million refugees) reporting that they had visited Ukraine at least once since their displacement2 Similarly, border monitoring interviews show that the incidence of repeated movements has also grown over time, as only 38% of individuals interviewed in the last quarter of 2023 were leaving the country for the first time, compared to 64% of those interviewed in last quarter of 2022.

Source: UNHCR's Intention Surveys

Source: UNHCR's Ukraine Border Montoring

How many refugees have returned to Ukraine?

The survey from UNHCR also shows that the majority of returns occurred in 2022, particularly from May to September, following the retaking of control of territories in northern oblasts. While the share of refugee returnees out of the total estimated population in Ukraine registered a peak of 4.6% in the surveys conducted in October 2022, it started to show a decreasing trend afterwards, reaching 3.4% in September 2023. While methodology and coverage of the survey has changed over time which can affect the comparison, this decrease can be explained by returnees who experienced secondary international displacements afterwards, as well as refugees who were returning only for short-term visits. Close to three quarters of returns took place toward Western, Northern and Eastern oblasts, and around half occurred from countries neighboring Ukraine, particularly from Poland (close to 40%), followed by Germany, Italy and the Czech Republic.

REFUGEES RETURNEES ESTIMATION BY ROUND OF DATA COLLECTION

Proportion of refugee returnees out of total estimated resident population in Ukraine at each round of data collection

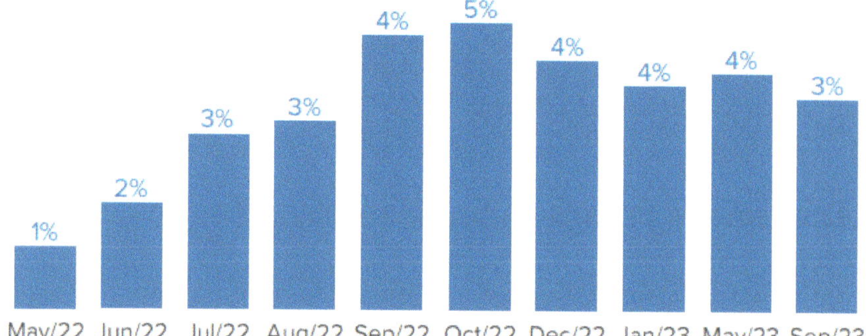

Source: UNHCR calculations based on IOM-Ukraine General Population Survey, R4-R14

Based on data from IOM's General Population Surveys (GPS) inside Ukraine, it is estimated that by September 2023 over 900,000 refugees from Ukraine had returned to their places of origin and remained in Ukraine for at least three months. Additionally, some 298,000 refugees are estimated to have returned to an area different from their former homes.

Paarth Mathur

How many refugees arrived in host countries in 2023?

MONTHLY DECISIONS GRANTING TEMPORARY PROTECTION IN EU+

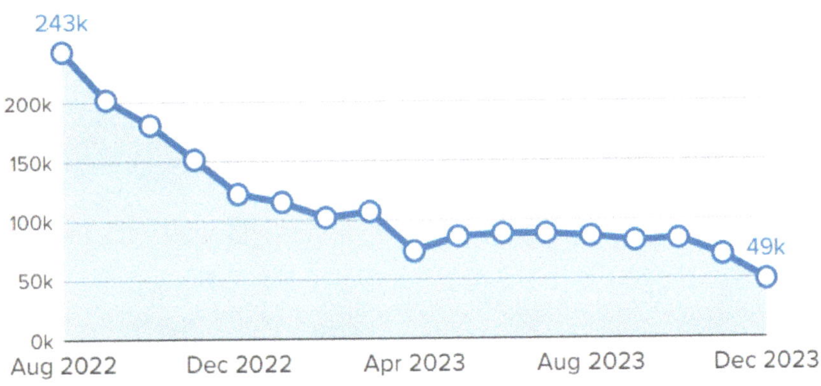

Source: EUROSTAT

     Similarly, to 2022, more than half of individuals granted TP in 2023 have been registered in Germany (25%), Poland (23%) and Czech Republic (10%). A slight change can be observed in the demographics compared to the beginning of the full-scale war, with an increase in the proportion of males of all ages among those granted temporary protection: from 34% in 2022 to 43% in 2023. It is worth mentioning that not all temporary protection decisions correspond to newly displaced refugees, as the figure can include re-applications or re-activations of previously granted cases, following a temporary visit to Ukraine. In fact, the total number of active beneficiaries of temporary protection increased by 525,000 persons between end-of 2022 and end-of 2023, which is around half of the total decisions granting TP during the year.

Voices: Linguistic and Cultural Dynamics of Refugee Population in America

According to data published by EUROSTAT, between January and December 2023, over 1,032,000 individuals were granted Temporary Protection (TP) in EU+ countries. While lower than in 2022, decisions granting temporary protection still average more than 87,000 per month, though with a decreasing trend during the year.6 Needs assessments recently conducted in ten refugee hosting countries show that around 14% of refugees arrived in 2023 to their current host countries.

How many refugees from Ukraine are currently in Europe and globally?

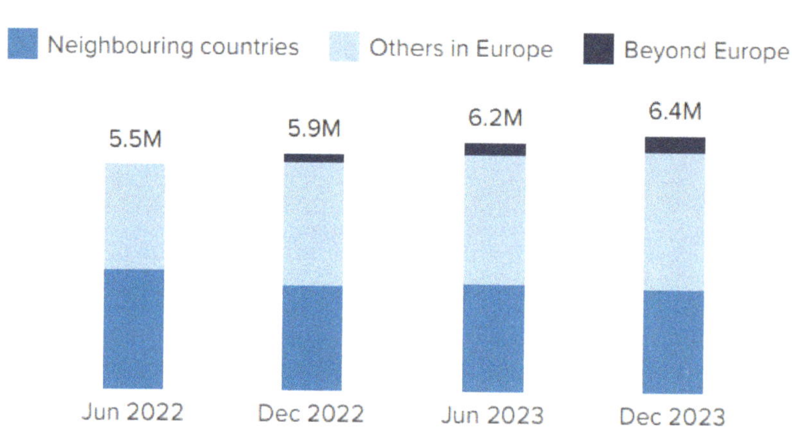

Source: Figures compiled by UNHCR based on data provided by authorities.

As of the end of 2023, close to 6.4 million refugees from Ukraine were recorded globally, including some 6.0 million hosted in countries across Europe.9 The number of refugees from Ukraine recorded in Europe has increased slightly in 2023 (+5%) compared to 2022 (5.7 million). While additional applications for temporary protection or asylum have been registered this year, and some countries have also reported new arrivals under other forms of stay, authorities in Europe have also adjusted their population estimates for different reasons (including de-deduplications and de-activations). On the other hand, onward movements outside of Europe have increased significantly in 2023, with over 403,600 refugees from Ukraine recorded outside of Europe by December 2023, compared to 230,000 by end of 2022. Most of these refugees are hosted in Canada and the United States of America, who have set-up specific schemes for temporary stay.

How many refugees from Ukraine are currently in United States?

In February 2024, the United States accepted 100 refugees from Ukraine. In fiscal year 2022 - which ended September 30, 2022 - the U.S. accepted a total of 1,610 Ukrainian refugees. The most Ukrainian refugees arrived in February of 2022, the same month that Ukraine was invaded by Russia.

In April 2022, the United States committed itself to welcoming 100,000 Ukrainian citizens and others fleeing Russian aggression in the region but has so far only accepted 2,402 since the Russian invasion in February last year.

Monthly intake of refugees from Ukraine to the United States from October 2021 to February 2024

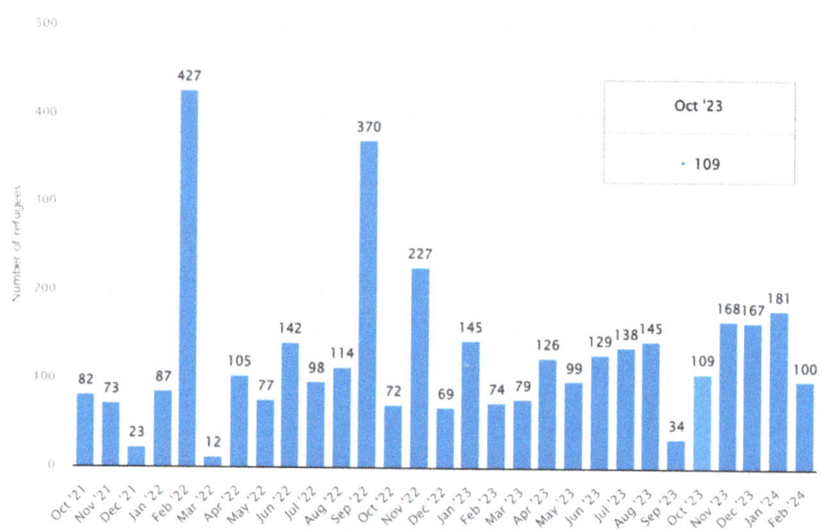

References

United Nations High Commissioner for Refugees. "Ukraine Refugee Situation." *UNHCR Data*, [publication date], https://data.unhcr.org/en/documents/details/106707?_gl=1*r58ljw*_rup_ga*MTgyMjY5OTQyNi4xNzEwMzgxNzIy*_rup_ga_EVDQTJ4LMY*MTcxMDM4MTcyMi4xLjEuMTcxMDM4Mjk4OC4xOC4wLjA.#_ga=2.40821856.350651536.1710381722-1822699426.1710381722. Accessed March 18, 2024

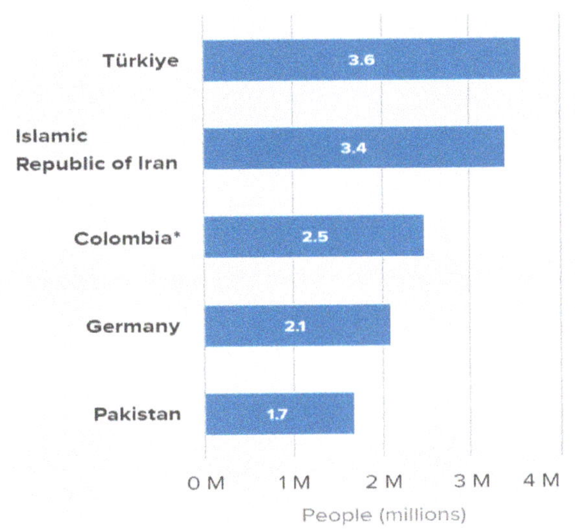

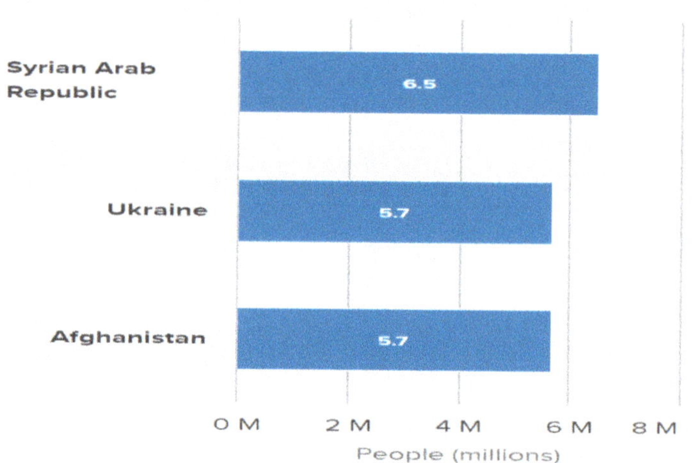
Major source countries
52 per cent of all refugees and other people in need of international protection came from just three countries.
Syrian Arab Republic
6.5
Ukraine
5.7
Afghanistan
5.7
0 M
2 M
4 M
6 M
8 M
People (millions)
14 June 2023
* Excludes Palestine refugees under UNRWA's mandate.
Source: UNHCR Global Trends 2022

52% originated from just three countries

52 per cent of all refugees and other people in need of international protection came from just three countries.

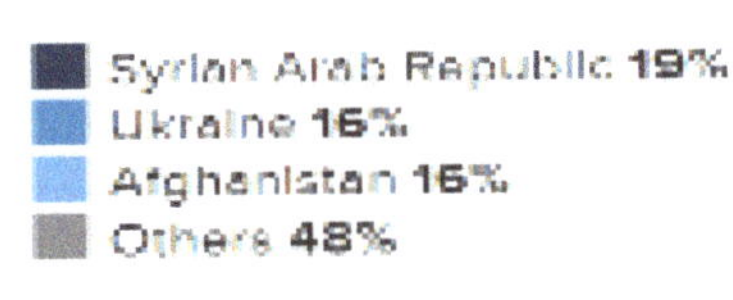

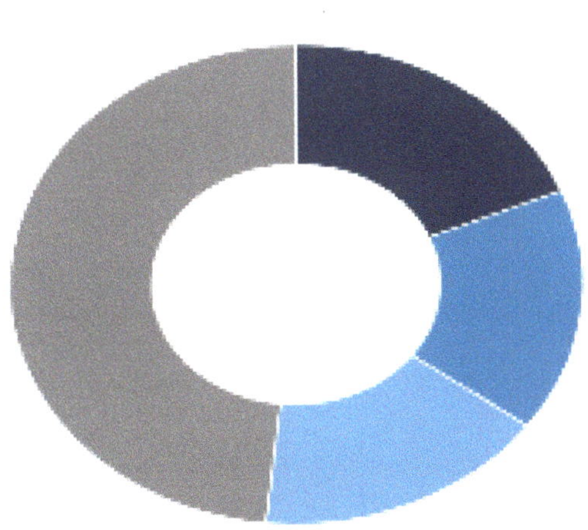

14 June 2023
Disclaimer: figures do not add up to 100 per cent due to rounding
* Excludes Palestine refugees under UNRWA's mandate
Source: UNHCR Global Trends 2022

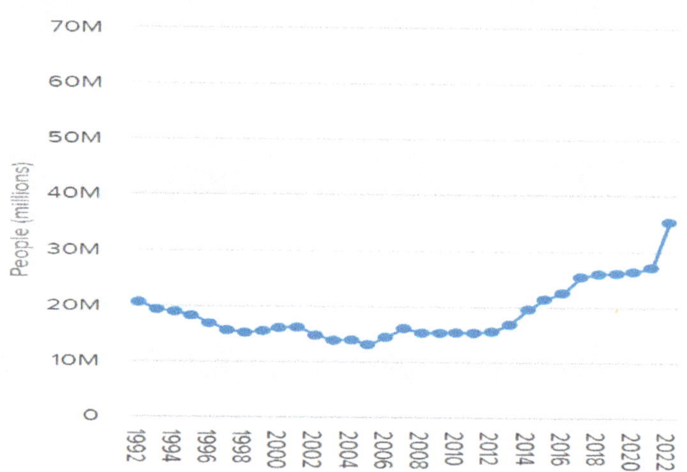
35.3 million refugees
29.4 million refugees under UNHCR's mandate.
5.9 million Palestine refugees under UNRWA's mandate.
70M
60M
50M
40M
30M
20M
10M
0
People (millions)
1992
1994
1996
1998
2000
2002
2004
2006
2008
2010
2012
2014
2016
2018
2020
2022
14 June 2023
Source: UNHCR Global Trends 2022

Paarth Mathur

108.4 million people worldwide were forcibly displaced

At the end of 2022 as a result of persecution, conflict, violence, human rights violations or events seriously disturbing public order.

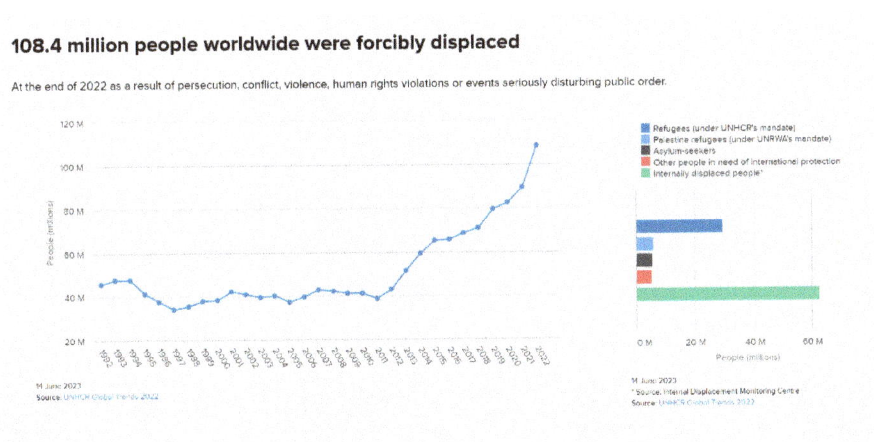

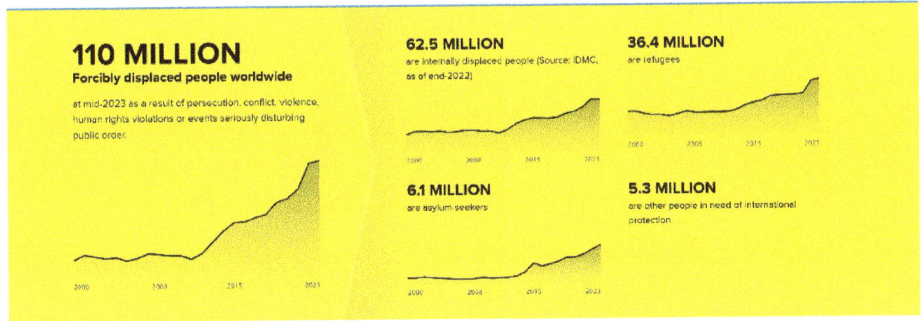

References

U.S. Census Bureau. "2010 American Community Survey." Integrated Public Use Microdata Series: Version 6.0. Compiled by Steven Ruggles, Katie Genadek, Ronald Goeken, Josiah Grover, and Matthew Sobek, University of Minnesota, 2012.

"1990 Decennial Census Summary Tape File 3." National Historical Geographic Information System: Version 2.0, University of Minnesota, 2013. Minnesota Population Center, University of Minnesota.

"2000 Decennial Census Summary File 4." National Historical Geographic Information System: Version 2.0, University of Minnesota, 2013. Minnesota Population Center, University of Minnesota.

"2015 American Community Survey." Public Use Microdata Series (PUMS) Data, U.S. Census Bureau, 2016. U.S. Census Bureau, Washington, DC.

United Nations High Commissioner for Refugees. "1951 Refugee Convention." UNHCR, https://www.unhcr.org/us/about-unhcr/who-we-are/1951-refugee-convention. Accessed [March 12, 2024].

International Rescue Committee. "Facts about Refugees: Key Facts, FAQs, and Statistics." International Rescue Committee, https://www.rescue.org/article/facts-about-refugees-key-facts-faqs-and-statistics. Accessed [March 10, 2024].

"LATINOS ARE TEXAS' LARGEST ETHNIC GROUP, BUT THAT DOESN'T EQUATE TO POLITICAL POWER." NPR, 11 Aug. 2023, https://www.npr.org/2023/08/11/1193534599/latinos-are-texas-largest-ethnic-group-but-that-doesnt-equate-to-political-power#:~:text=group%20in%20Texas.-,But%20experts%20say%20this%20population%20growth%20is%2

0a%20long%20way,to%20the%20U.S.%20Census%20Bureau. Accessed March 12,2024

"Bridging Refugee Youth and Children's Services (BRYCS)." Cultural Adjustment, Integration Barriers & Perspectives from Refugee Youth, Bridging Refugee Youth and Children's Services, https://brycs.org/youth-development/cultural-adjustment-integration-barriers-perspectives-from-refugee-youth/#:~:text=Struggling%20with%20cultural%20adjustment%20can,%2C%20activities%2C%20and%20the%20community. Accessed Feb 02, 2024

Bridging Refugee Youth and Children's Services. BRYCS RYC Trees Flow Chart. Aug. 2018, https://brycs.org/wp-content/uploads/2018/08/brycs-ryc-trees-flow-chart.pdf. Accessed Feb 12,2024

Beauchamp, Zack. "Refugees in the United States, Explained." Vox, Vox Media, 14 June 2022, https://www.vox.com/future-perfect/2022/6/14/23162982/refugees-united-states-displaced-people-afghanistan-ukraine-biden-trump. Accessed Feb 12,2024

Sirin, Selcuk R., and Lauren Rogers-Sirin. "The Educational and Mental Health Needs of Syrian Refugee Children." Migration Policy Institute, vol. 15, no. 4, Oct. 2015, https://www.ncbi.nlm.nih.gov/pmc/articles/PMC3856769/. Accessed Dec 16,2023

West, Brady T., and Jennifer Van Hook. "How Well Do You Speak English? Assessing the Validity of the American Community Survey English Ability Question." Research Matters, U.S. Census Bureau, 23 Oct. 2015,

https://www.census.gov/newsroom/blogs/research-matters/2015/10/how-well-do-you-speak-english-assessing-the-validity-of-the-american-community-survey-english-ability-question.html. Accessed Dec 16, 2023

Siggnn. "Diversity in Sign Languages: The Global Linguistic Tapestry." LinkedIn, LinkedIn, [Publication Date], https://www.linkedin.com/pulse/diversity-sign-languages-global-linguistic-tapestry-siggnn/. Accessed March 17, 2024

"Sign Language Linguistics." Deaf Websites, https://deafwebsites.com/sign-language-linguistics/. Accessed March 18,2024

"Tulane University School of Public Health and Tropical Medicine." "Cultural Competence in Health Care." Tulane University School of Public Health and Tropical Medicine, https://publichealth.tulane.edu/blog/cultural-competence-in-health-care/#:~:text=What%20Is%20Cultural%20Competence%20in,attitud es%2C%20values%2C%20and%20behaviors. Accessed March 23,2024